The Great Train Robbery, an Edison film directed by Edwin S. Porter in 1903, is the first Western in the history of the cinema.

The bandits attack the telegraph office at the station,

kill the post office worker, dynamite the mail car's safe,

knock out the driver, and bring the train to a stop,

They steal the luggage and shoot someone trying to escape

before getting away on the locomotive with the booty

They ride off on horseback.

The telegraph operator is rescued by his daughter

and runs to alert the men gathered in the saloon.

A chase ensues, and one of the bandits is mortally wounded.

When the remaining bandits stop to divide up the booty,

they are encircled, and every one of them is killed.

CONTENTS

BIRTH OF THE
MOTION PICTURE

Emmanuelle Toulet

DISCOVERIES

HARRY N. ABRAMS, INC., PUBLISHERS

"Are you free tonight?"

"Yes," I replied, "why do you ask?"

"Come to the Grand Café at nine o'clock. You amaze everyone with your tricks, but you are going to see something that may amaze even you!"

"Really? What is it?"

"Shh," he said, "just come and you'll see. It'll be worth it, but I don't want to give anything away."

CHAPTER I
THE BEGINNING OF A NEW WORLD

Top hats, cocked hats, military caps, flat hats of priests, and round hats of children—all crowded the narrow entrance to the Salon Indien. According to the first cinema poster (1896, opposite), designed by Henri Brispot, the Lumière Cinématographe was one attraction whose mystery conflicted with neither good taste nor morals. Right: From *Bataille de Femmes* (*Battle of the Women*).

CINÉMATOGRAPHE LUMIÈRE

The second poster for the Cinématographe, made around 1896, shows the hall and the spectators' enjoyment of *L'Arroseur Arrosé* (*The Sprinkler Sprinkled*, 1895).

One evening in December 1895, Antoine Lumière entered the office of the magician Georges Méliès at the Robert-Houdin Theater in Paris to present him with this mysterious invitation. A bohemian and extravagant character whose adventures had begun with the founding of a photographic studio in Lyon, Lumière had come to Paris to take charge of the public presentation of the latest invention of his two sons, Auguste and Louis, who were serious, hardworking, and ingenious young men.

Some members of the crowd, afraid of being crushed by the locomotive they saw bearing down on them, ran away or shrunk into their seats. Below is a sketch for a poster attributed to Jules Chéret, which was never made.

28 December 1895: The First Public Showing of the Cinématographe

Georges Méliès would never forget that evening: "The other guests and I found ourselves in front of a small screen, similar to those we use for…projections, and, after a few minutes, a stationary photograph showing the Place Bellecour in Lyon was projected. A little surprised, I scarcely had time to say to my neighbor: 'Is it just to have us see projections that he has brought us here? I've been doing them for ten years.'

"No sooner had I stopped speaking when a horse pulling a cart started to walk toward us, followed by other vehicles, then passersby—in short, the whole vitality of a street. We were open-mouthed, dumbfounded, astonished beyond words in the face of this spectacle."

The Cinématographe had already been shown to the scientific world at private meetings. Would public showings with an admission charge appeal to Parisians, for whom, at the end of the century, there was no shortage of novelties? Would they be attracted to the obscure, newfangled name with which the apparatus was baptized? Clément Maurice, a former employee of the Lumière company, organized the public screenings. He rented the Salon Indien, a small hall in the basement of the Grand Café at 14 Boulevard des Capucines. The setup was nothing if not basic: a cloth screen, a hundred chairs, a projector placed on a stool, and, at the entrance, a hawker announcing "Lumière Cinématographe, Admission One Franc."

The shows in the Salon Indien, at the Grand Café (above), lasted until 1901, but after 1896 other sites, for the most part located along the same thoroughfare, were used increasingly for screenings. The old "Boulevard of Crime," the location of the popular 19th-century theater, became the "Boulevard of Cinema."

The First Curiosity Seekers Who Had Come in by Chance Spread Their Enthusiasm: Soon There Was a Crowd at the Entrance to the Salon Indien

The first day, 28 December 1895, there was little success, with only thirty-three spectators; the press, though invited, could not be bothered to attend. But after a few days, with no advertising other than word of mouth, there were crowds galore. "Those who decided to come in left a little bewildered," recalled Clément Maurice. "Then, shortly after, you saw them come back, bringing along all the acquaintances they could find on the boulevard." Before long, more than two thousand spectators were rushing to the door of the Salon Indien each day, and mobs were forming—sometimes fights even broke out. The police had to move in to maintain order.

A piano was soon installed in the dark hall to drown out the creaking sound of the machine. The twenty-minute program consisted of ten films, and viewers all

L'Arrivée d'un Train à la Ciotat (*The Arrival of a Train at a Station*) was filmed in 1895 by Louis Lumière, who placed his camera on the edge of the platform and began to turn its crank when the train from Marseilles appeared on the horizon. While the passengers wait, the locomotive approaches, grows larger and larger, and finally exits screen left. The single-shot sequence lasts for fifty seconds.

Salle des Dépêches du PROGRÈS
85, RUE DE LA RÉPUBLIQUE, 85

Le Cinématographe
LUMIÈRE

Semaine du 12 au 18 Juin 1898

VUES PROJETÉES :

PANORAMA OU CHEMIN DE FER A L'ENTRÉE DU TUNNEL DE PERRACHE

1. Passage dans le tunnel.
2. Sortie du tunnel.
3. Les Maçons.
4. Un prêté pour un rendu.
5. Régates militaires en Autriche (Aller).
6. — (Retour).
7. Transport d'une locomotive de Lyon à Francheville.
8. L'Amoureux dans le sac.

LES SÉANCES ONT LIEU

Tous les Jours et les Dimanches et Fêtes
De 2 h. à 6 h. 1/2 et de 8 h. 1/2 à 10 h. 1/2.

Prix d'Entrée : 50 centimes.

L'ENTRE-SOL
Rayons X Expériences scientifiques et publiques,

Visibles tous les jours, de 2 h. à 6 h. 1/2 et de 8 h. à 11 h.
ENTRÉE : 50 CENTIMES.

exhibited the same reactions: skeptical or blasé at the appearance of a static photographic projection, stupefied when it became animated, admiring at the sight of the wind in the trees and the agitation of the waves, and afraid when the train entering the station at La Ciotat seemed to throw itself at them. By the end they were enthusiastic.

Plunged into the dark, eyes strained by the flickering light, the jumping image, and the jerky rapidity of any movement, the members of the audience did not feel they were present at the beginnings of a new form of spectacle. The Cinématographe seemed to them cut out for a profound but different calling: the reproduction of life—and maybe its resurrection, as one journalist's reaction bears witness: "When these gadgets are in the hands of the public, when anyone can photograph the ones who are dear to them, not just in their immobile form, but with movement, action, familiar gestures, and the words out of their mouths, then death will no longer be absolute, final."

Motion-picture projections took place in Lyon on the occasion of a congress of French photographic societies starting in June 1895. A permanent cinema was functioning in its inventors' hometown by January of the next year.

From the start Louis Lumière proved to be a master director. His talents as a designer and photographer certainly inspired his sense of framing, spacing, and lighting. Scenes of daily life, often shot with members of his family, mix spontaneity and staging, as the 1895 *Leçon de Bicyclette* (*Bicycle Lesson*, below) shows.

The Cinématographe soon toured the capitals of Europe. In London after a first public screening on 20 February 1896 at Marlborough Hall, the Cinématographe was installed at the Empire Theatre (opposite), where it attracted full houses starting with its opening on 9 March 1896. Screenings in England (poster, above left) were organized by Félicien Trewey, a French magician and shadow illusionist famous in England who was a friend of Antoine Lumière's. In *La Partie d'Écarté* (*The Card Game*), filmed in 1895 by Louis Lumière (below left), Trewey, in the middle, plays cards with the father and father-in-law of the director. While Trewey's incursion into the world of the motion picture was fleeting, his collaborator, Matt Raymond, a young English electrician, was responsible for the increased number of projectors installed in England and Ireland and would remain an important figure in the development of the cinema in Great Britain.

**New York, 29 June 1896:
The Acclaim of the American
Public**

Auguste and Louis Lumière decided not to sell
their device, as everyone was demanding. Instead, they
chose to exploit it themselves by sending abroad
operators who were entrusted with a double
mission: to shoot films to be shown by the
Cinématographe and to rent halls and
organize screenings. Demand was
enormous, and competition loomed
on every front.

In May 1896 Félix
Mesguich, a new
recruit to the firm, set
sail for the United
States. The first American
screening of the Cinématographe took place on
29 June 1896 in a
New York music hall,
Keith's Vaudeville Theatre, in
front of a crowd of eager viewers. "You had to have lived
these moments of collective exaltation, have attended

The catalogues and lists of Lumière films offered, between 1895 and 1907, 1424 "views" divided into 337 war scenes, 247 foreign trips, 175 trips inside France, 181 official celebrations, 125 French military views, 97 comic films, 63 "panoramas," 61 maritime scenes, 55 foreign military views, 46 dances, and 37 popular festivals. The image at left is from *Parade de Sport* (*Sports Exhibition*).

these thrilling screenings in order to understand just how far the excitement of the crowd could go," said Mesguich. "With a flick of a switch, I plunge several thousand spectators into darkness. Each scene passes, accompanied by tempestuous applause; after the sixth scene, I return the hall to light. The audience is shaking. Cries ring out: 'The Lumière Brothers, the Lumière Brothers!'" Mesguich would also remember having been beset by journalists and carried in triumph while an orchestra played "La Marseillaise," the French national anthem.

The "city portraits" made by Lumière operators, like this view of Chicago and its ferris wheel, were intended for a dual audience—spectators eager to discover foreign countries and customs and local viewers who took pleasure in recognizing familiar places.

"America for Americans"

As word of the Cinématographe spread, people were getting impatient. Each town demanded screenings, and each week the small firm from Lyon sent new operators, who were immediately deluged with work. The French could not keep up with the demand indefinitely.

Competition was hot. In the business climate fostered by President William McKinley, rival devices surged onto the market, often accompanied by the slogan "America for Americans." One unabashedly patriotic advertisement read: "The images of the American Biograph do not shake like those of the Cinématographe. The Biograph projects a much larger image than the French one. And besides, it is an American machine. So there will be more views of a national character."

The Lumière operators ran up against new worries in the United States. In January 1897, while filming a snowball fight in the streets, Mesguich was arrested and taken to the police station on the pretext that he did not have the proper authorization.

Five months later the Customs Service was on the company's trail, alleging that equipment was coming into the country illegally. Agents seized French projectors, and the Lumière branch director fled on a transatlantic ship.

Thus the American adventures of the Lumière Cinématographe—an ephemeral episode of only one year—came to an end, like a dream ending in a brutal awakening. However, the harvest of films shot by the company's operators during their wanderings, which took them from the New York City subway to Niagara Falls, did survive.

In his memoirs, *Tours de Manivelle* (*Cranking the Camera,* 1933), Félix Mesguich recounts his travels in the service of the Lumières in France, the United States, Canada, and Russia. A man with a calling, a pioneer of both advertising films and the talkies, he was, in his own words, "an image chaser."

St. Petersburg: The Crowning of the Czar and a Terrible Tragedy

Czar Nicholas II, who had succeeded Alexander III two years previously, was to be crowned on 14 May 1896. This exceptional subject attracted Lumière operators to Russia. For this reason, films were shot in Russia before any public screenings took place.

Intervention by the French embassy was necessary to overcome the government's distrust of the Cinématographe, which, when it was in operation, sounded like the ticking of a bomb. To house Lumière

Seven films shot by Charles Moisson and Francis Doublier on the occasion of the crowning of the czar are listed in the Lumière catalogue. This one shows the sovereigns and guests on their way to the annointing.

operators Charles Moisson and Francis Doublier and
their equipment, a special stand was built; from here
the first Russian films, ceremonial images of the last
of the czars, were recorded. And the camera was there
two days later, when the sovereign was presented to
the people and a balustrade gave way. Panic took
hold of the crowd of almost a half-million people;
people were trampled, and the police charged those
who came near the imperial rostrum. What was the
reaction of the operators to this terrible scene? They
continued to turn the camera crank. They were soon
arrested by the police, and their equipment was
confiscated. No one would ever see their footage of
five thousand dead bodies, but a new concept of
journalism had been born.

The first public screening in Russia took place on 17
May at the Aquarium, St. Petersburg's summer theater.
The arrival of a train—always the most striking scene—
took on added resonance in the country of the novelist
Leo Tolstoy: "When on the horizon a whole train rushed
at us, when it seemed to break through the screen, our
minds immediately called up the same scene in *Anna
Karenina*," noted an educated witness.

On 7 July the Lumière program, presented by Eugène
Promio, made a conquest of the czar and the court.
The brothers Arthur and Ivan Grünewald won the
Russian franchise for the Cinématographe and engaged
the most adventurous young French operators in a tour
of all the Russias. The Cinématographe touched every
audience. At one fair, it evoked both the terror and
anger of the peasants, who wondered, "Was it sorcery
or political propaganda?" The operator got back to
his hotel under police protection, but the hall and the
machine were torched.

This incident may be contrasted with a high-society
scandal of the following year. Félix Mesguich filmed a
famous Spanish dancer, "The Beautiful Otero," dancing
with a Russian officer at a gala evening. At the screening,
the cameraman was arrested and accused of having
offended the Army and was quickly thrown out of the
country without further ado.

An 1899 Russian poster
(below): "For the last
time! In Tambov, with
the permission of the
authorities…a showing of
the Lumière Cinéma-
tographe will take place."

This Italian program combined three attractions that would be closely linked until the dawn of the 20th century: X rays (discovered by Wilhelm Conrad Röntgen in 1895), panoramas, and the motion picture.

Gorky's "Kingdom of Shadows": "The Strangeness of This World"

Paris, New York, St. Petersburg: three places of the many in which the Cinématographe appeared, three destinies.

The future did not look bright to all. Behind the praise for this new step in the progress of humanity lurked an unease, vividly felt by the Russian writer Maksim Gorky, for example, when he discovered the Lumière Cinématographe at a fair in Nizhni-Novgorod: "Last evening, I was in the Kingdom of the Shadows. If one could only convey the strangeness of this world. A world without color and sound. Everything here—the earth, water, and air, the trees, the people—everything is made of a monotone gray. Gray rays of sunlight in a gray sky, gray eyes in a gray face, leaves as gray as cinder. Not life, but the shadow of life. Not life's movement, but a sort of mute specter."

After having traveled across Latin America and Japan, Lumière camera operator Gabriel Veyre went to China in 1899. Filming in the streets provoked varied reactions, evidence of which remains visible on film: thus, this fan in the foreground. Sometimes passersby approach the lens curiously until they block its view, or amused children stand in the field of vision and point out the camera with a finger.

Actograph, Andersonoscopograph, Animatograph, Biactograph, Biograph, Bioscope, Bioskop, Cameragraph, Choreutoscope, Chronophotographe, Cinématographe, Eidoloscope, Eknetograph, Electrograph, Fregoligraph, Iconograph, Kineopticon, Kinetograph, Kinetoscope, Mutoscope, Panoptikon, Phantascope, Phototachygraph, Polyscope, Scenematograph, Thaumatograph, Theatrograph, Vitascope…

CHAPTER II

INVENTION AFTER INVENTION

Opposite: *La Danse du Diable* (*The Dance of the Devil*, c. 1904). In around 1870 Antoine Lumière posed with his photographic equipment (right).

After 1890 Devices for the Recording and Projection of Moving Pictures Came Thick and Fast, but Some Problems Remained Unsolved

One invention led to another. Experimenters who didn't even know about each other's work sometimes obtained identical results. Five years passed in feverish excitement, with a general sense of urgency and secrecy. That any given invention was created before any other is sometimes difficult to establish, and there is another problem: How can we know if an apparatus, for which the patents are not always explicit, actually functioned, and if the product was of good quality? Also, what were the stumbling blocks around 1890?

The analysis of motion in a series of sequential photographs had already been achieved. Eadweard Muybridge, a British photographer working in California, and Etienne-Jules Marey, a French physiologist, had arrived at results of startling clarity. Further, Marey had the idea of recording images on a long strip of photographic paper that unrolled in front of the lens instead of on separate plates—but his device had no way to ensure that the movement of the strip would be regular.

In 1893 Albert Londe, an employee of a hospital for the mentally ill, made these "successive photographs" of a tightrope walker with a multiple-lens apparatus he had built to study nervous diseases.

Georges Démeny, an associate of Marey's, developed the Phonoscope (left and above) to demonstrate lip movements to deaf-mutes to help them learn to speak.

The apparatus for recording images—the motion-picture camera—was also being developed. After Muybridge, who made his sequential photographs by using a series of individual cameras, some inventors built prototypes with multiple lenses; others were moving toward cameras with a single lens. The main challenge was to synchronize the movement of the raw material upon which the image would be recorded with the opening of the lens shutter.

In Germany in 1887 Ottomar Anschütz was able to re-create movement with a device using transparent chronophotographs, the Electrotachyscope.

The search for an apparatus to resynthesize motion—a projector—however, was less advanced. The basic principle— that a material able to be exposed had to be run past a light source— was widely understood. But in order for movement to be accurately resynthesized, the number of images illuminated in a second had to be identical to the number of images recorded in the same time period.

Eadweard James Muybridge

In 1872 the well-known photographer Muybridge, an Englishman who had emigrated to the United States, began his studies of animal locomotion by photographing horses, at the behest of Leland Stanford, who owned a major stable. Using the same technique, he studied other animals, aligning twelve, twenty-four, and then forty cameras mounted with electromagnetic shutters timed to go off one after the other. By projecting these sequential snapshots, he could reconstruct movement. Later on, Muybridge analyzed the movements of the human body.

Etienne-Jules Marey

Marey studied the movement of animals, which led to his interest in photography. To understand the flight of birds, in 1882 he developed a photographic gun with which he obtained twelve images on a circular plate. He perfected his system by constructing a Chrono-photographe using rolls of paper film. He was able to deconstruct movement by photo-graphing against a black background; first he photographed men in white (opposite above), followed by men in black clothing carrying white sticks (left). Unlike Muybridge, Marey was not concerned with putting the images back together to reconstruct movement.

So the feed mechanism played a vital role, and it is on this critical point that a solution was most eagerly awaited in the 1890s.

The Most Enigmatic of the Unlucky Inventors of Cinema

On 16 September 1890 a man who had boarded the express train for Paris at Dijon, in eastern France, disappeared without a trace. No explanation would ever be found. The man was called Louis Aimé Augustin Le Prince. In 1888 he had constructed a camera with sixteen lenses behind which two strips of film advanced intermittently. In the next year or two, he experimented with a camera equipped with a single lens, a projector with a Maltese cross—a metal part that regulates the intermittent advancing of the film—and a filmstrip made of perforated celluloid, and he managed to shoot several sequences. So all the ingredients for the motion picture were in place. If the inventor hadn't mysteriously disappeared, might the cinema have been born five years earlier?

Edison Tried to Produce an "Instrument that Does for the Eye What the Phonograph Does for the Ear"

During an 1888 lecture tour in which he displayed his experiments on human and animal locomotion with a Zoopraxiscope, Eadweard Muybridge stopped off in West Orange, New Jersey. There Muybridge met Thomas Alva Edison, a young man who had already applied for nearly a hundred patents, and who was becoming particularly well known for such noteworthy inventions as the telegraph, the incandescent lamp, and the phonograph.

Fred Ott, who worked for Edison, performs his specialty in front of the Kinetograph. *Fred Ott's Sneeze* (opposite right) was the first film ever officially copyrighted, on 7 January 1894. The strip ran in a continuous loop on the Kinetoscope (below).

The Universal Expositions of 1889 and 1900 were the occasion of fruitful contacts among three major figures in the history of motion pictures, Edison (above left), Dickson (opposite left), and Marey (opposite center).

It was shortly after this meeting that the prolific young inventor conceived of a motion-picture recording device based on the model of the cylinder he had already used to construct a sound-recording machine. He assigned the job of studying two apparatuses—one for the recording of images, baptized the Kinetograph, and the other for viewing them, named the Kinetoscope—to an employee with a passion for photography, the Englishman William Kennedy Laurie Dickson. The two men proceeded cautiously. Arriving in Paris for the Universal Exposition of 1889, Edison met Marey, who told him about the progress of his own work. Eventually, in order to record photographic views, the American inventor abandoned the cylinder for a celluloid roll with perforations (sprocket holes) along each side, through which a toothed sprocket wheel would run; this ensured a uniform feed.

In His West Orange Laboratories, Edison Constructed the Kinetoscope

In 1889 George W. Eastman, of the company that is still known as Eastman Kodak, had begun to sell a new kind of flexible and transparent photographic material made of cellulose nitrate. (This roll film had been developed by the Reverend Hannibal Goodwin.) When William Dickson ordered some 35-mm-wide strips of this material from the Eastman factories, one could say that "film" was invented.

In 1891 the Kinetoscope was perfected: It was a large cabinet with a peephole through which one viewed an animated scene recorded on a continuous loop of film. It did not allow for projection on a screen; it was purely for individual viewing. Three years later these new, coin-operated machines were made available to the public and would become another claim to fame for Edison, the "wizard of West Orange."

Meanwhile, Dickson Made Films in the Black Maria, the World's First Motion-Picture Studio, and the Business of the Moving Image Took Shape

To supply the Kinetoscopes with material to show, Dickson assumed the job of recording films with the Kinetograph. Daylight was seldom sufficient for this task, so in 1893 a curious device was added to the installation at West Orange—a sort of misshapen black shed the employees nicknamed the Black Maria, the slang term for a paddy wagon. The world's first movie studio, equipped with a roof that opened, was built on a railroad turntable, so it could rotate to capture the sunlight all day long.

Filming went on ceaselessly. The firm's employees, including Dickson himself,

"No dungeons are these, thrilling with awful possibilities, but simply a building for the better taking of kinetographic subjects [the Black Maria, below].... No department of the wizard's domains is more fraught with perennial interest than this theatre; none are more interwoven with the laughter, the pathos, the genius and the dexterities of life. No earthly stage has ever gathered within its precincts a more incongruous crew of actors since the days when gods and men and animals were on terms of social intimacy. "
William Kennedy Laurie Dickson,
History of the Photographic and Scientific Experiments and Developments Leading up to the Perfection of the Vitascope, 1896

Dickson shot *Fun in a Chinese Laundry* in 1894 in the Black Maria. This film features a rudimentary set in front of a black background and a rough attempt at direction. It lasts only thirty seconds.

were the first to venture in front of the black tarpaper backing that served as a set. But soon actors, athletes, and artists from Barnum and Bailey's Circus and Buffalo Bill's Wild West Show were all performing there. Theatrical companies came to record a few scenes from their most recent successes. Dickson staged scenarios of his own invention and also shot, outside the Black Maria, a few films in the open air.

To make scenes one minute long that curiosity seekers would watch through a peephole for the price of a nickel, performers grimaced, sneezed,

Kinetoscopes were placed at the public's disposal in special parlors, at markets, and at fairgrounds around the world. Above: A Swiss poster.

Peter Bacigalupi's Phonograph and Kinetoscope Parlor in San Francisco (left, 1894) was one of many establishments that made the new inventions available to the public for a fee.

gesticulated, acted, danced, and boxed. A first film of boxing found such success that a fight pitting the world heavyweight champion, "Gentleman Jim" Corbett, against Peter Courtney was specially organized for the movies and was promoted with an enormous press campaign. Boxing matches played an important role in the development of the early cinema; they drew outside capital and generated unusually long films.

Edison, the farsighted inventor, was a businessman of genius, to whom the Kinetoscope brought unforeseen profits. The first Kinetoscope parlor opened in New York on 14 April 1894. Others sprang up in the large American cities, as well as in London, Paris, and Mexico. The sale of machines and of films was entrusted by franchise to a few agents. Motion pictures had already become the basis of a lucrative international trade.

Max Skladanowsky, the German Father of the Motion Picture?

While the American credit for the invention of the motion picture goes to Edison, and the French credit is taken by the Lumière brothers, Germans consider that the glory can be equally well granted to one of their own.

The father of Max and Emil Skladanowsky was a specialist in optical entertainment; he put on shows with a "magic lantern," an early form of the slide projector. His sons took over the business and went on tour around northern and central Europe with "transformation scenes" produced by lanterns equipped with multiple lenses. As a businessman concerned with keeping his show fresh, Max Skladanowsky took series of photographic shots on celluloid film, then worked for three years on the construction of an enormous projector, the Bioskop, which featured two film strips, perforated with metallic eyelets, which ran in parallel and were exposed alternately.

On 1 November 1895—fifty-eight days before the performances at the Grand Café in Paris—the first public projection of the Bioskop took place, at the Wintergarden in Berlin. The Skladanowskys' show was distinguished by the organization and content of its program, composed exclusively of vaudeville acts ranging from the Boxing Kangaroo to the Snake Dance, with each scene preceded by the projection of its title with a magic lantern dissolve. In 1896 the two Skladanowsky brothers left on a tour of the capitals of northern Europe. But only rarely were they the first to arrive, and the Bioskop, with its limited possibilities—it was a very complicated device—could not survive in what was already becoming a crowded and competitive motion-picture market.

A true craftsman of the cinema, Max Skladanowsky built his camera and cut, assembled, and perforated his film himself. The Bioskop simultaneously used two bands of forty-eight images each, running at a speed of eight frames a second. The length of each projection was under ten seconds. A sequence from one of his films is above.

"Of All My Inventions, This One Has Cost Me the Least," Louis Lumière Liked to Say

Certainly, the two sons of the Lyon photographer were very bright fellows. After scientific and practical studies at the Ecole de la Martinière, the elder, Auguste, and Louis worked in their father's firm, which had just added a small factory for making photographic plates to the photographic studio. In 1881, when he was seventeen years old, Louis developed a "dry plate" made of a very sensitive gelatin emulsion; its success would ensure the fortunes of the Lumière family. A new factory was established in the Montplaisir quarter of Lyon. By 1894 the Lumière company employed three hundred workers and produced fifteen million "blue label" photographic plates.

The young industrialists remained, despite their prosperity, researchers in spirit; they investigated questions of biology, color photography, and moving pictures. Focusing on the latter, Auguste built several unsuccessful devices. Then the brothers visited the Edison franchise store in Paris. They examined the Kinetoscopes and were inspired to continue their own experiments. First they adopted the American machine's perforated film, but the delicate problem of its advancement remained. Then, one night, toward the end of 1894...

"I Was Rather Indisposed and Had to Remain in Bed. One Night When I Was Unable to Sleep, the Solution Came Clearly to My Mind"

"The solution consisted of adapting for the camera the mechanism known by the name of 'presser foot' in the drive device of sewing machines," recounted Louis Lumière.

"In one night, my brother invented the Cinématographe," his brother said.

Charles Moisson, then the head machinist at the factory, was entrusted with the task of building a prototype. It seemed immediately satisfying; its features would enjoy an astonishingly long life. Unquestionably practical, it was lightweight, compact, and served as well for the shooting and printing of films as for their projection. It ran at sixteen frames per second, a speed that

Lumière jumps over a chair to show how fast his dry-plate process was.

would turn out to be commonly used until the arrival of the talkies in 1929. It utilized Edison's film, that celluloid strip 35 mm in width, the only difference being that while the Kinetoscope film had four lateral rectangular perforations on each frame, each frame of the Lumière film had only a single round one on each side. As for the feed mechanism—the brainstorm of that night of insomnia—it allowed for the intermittent movement of the film and, by synchronizing the opening of the shutter with the moment the film paused, enabled enlarged images to be projected on a screen.

In 1895 Louis Lumière had only one camera, a prototype built by Charles Moisson, with which he had recorded his first film, *La Sortie d'Usine* (*Workers Leaving the Lumière Factory*). Near the end of the year, he ordered a model that included numerous improvements (above). The emulsion on the film was the same as that used on the "blue label" plates, which explains the remarkably high photographic quality of the Lumière films.

SOCIÉTÉ LUMIÈRE

PLAQUES AU GÉLATINO-BROMURE D'ARGENT

A. LUMIÈRE & SES FILS

EXTRA RAPIDES

Although Louis alone was the creator of the invention, the two brothers together signed the patent application on 13 February 1895, as was their custom. Antoine Lumière, confident of his sons' genius, suggested naming the device Domitor, a swaggering Latinism, but Louis and Auguste preferred the more scientific-sounding Hellenic term Cinématographe.

At the 1900 exposition (poster below), motion pictures were considered a branch of photography. Lumière, Gaumont, and others presented cameras, film, and a variety of equipment.

Obsessed with the Idea of "Total Cinema," Louis Lumière Imagined a Giant Cinématographe

"The guiding myth inspiring the invention of cinema," wrote the postwar French critic André Bazin, "is the accomplishment of that which dominated in a more-or-less vague fashion all the techniques of the mechanical reproduction of reality in the 19th century, from photography to the phonograph—namely, an integral realism, a re-creation of the world in its own image, an image unburdened by the freedom of interpretation of the artist or the irreversibility of time. If cinema in its cradle lacked all the attributes of the cinema to come, it was reluctantly and because its fairy guardians were unable to provide them, however much they would have liked to."

His whole life, Louis Lumière, a passionate experimenter, pursued the idea of a total cinema by researching projection, sound, color, and stereoscopy. This quest reached a particularly high intensity at the turn of the century—and by then Lumière was hardly the only one engaged in it.

In anticipation of the 1900 Universal Exposition in Paris, the inventor became interested in the possibility of enlarging the film's projected image; this interest in the gigantic was commensurate with the universality and the excess of the huge world's fair.

The Universal Exposition had the proclaimed ambition of being the executor of the legacy of the century gone by and the oracle of the century being born: Film would have a prominent place there. Invited separately from the many private motion-picture companies flourishing at the fair, the giant Lumière Cinématographe enjoyed a position there that represented the official recognition of the cinema and the personal consecration of its inventors—a consecration that pushed rivals aside.

The giant-screen Cinématographe featured a program of fifteen cinematographic scenes and fifteen color photographs, in a show that lasted a half hour. In total, 150 different films were screened.

At the 1900 Universal Exposition, 1.5 Million Spectators Gazed at a Screen of Almost 500 Square Yards

The first plan had been to hang a vast screen on the Eiffel Tower, but technical difficulties meant that this open-air theater had to be scrapped. Instead, the giant Cinématographe was installed in the exposition's huge

Festival Hall, which could accommodate fifteen thousand spectators; it had been the Gallery of Machines in the 1889 fair.

The screen, about seventy feet wide and sixty feet high, was stored in a tank of water under the floor and hauled up each evening by powerful winches while jets of water sprinkled it; the projection's luminosity was enhanced by the dampness of the cloth. The show could be viewed from both sides of the screen.

Over six months, 326 free performances gave the newborn attraction an unprecedented impact. Despite its success, though, the experience would not be repeated. After this time, the focus shifted to the representation of space and the achievement of dramatic intensity within the frame of the image.

Reproducing the Colors of Life

Several techniques for coloring film—both manual and mechanical—were used at this time. Exhibitors had a choice between renting a given motion picture in black and white or in its more expensive color version. Only the most sumptuous and the most carefully prepared subjects, like "fairy films" and trick films, were automatically entitled to the luxury color treatment, which sometimes involved only a few scenes.

The first method was hand tinting each print of a film, frame by frame. To produce the best effect, the shooting had to be done with this in mind: In order for the image to offer the necessary translucency, the backdrops, props, costumes, and makeup would have to be a monotone

"I employed two hundred women in my studio. I spent my evenings selecting and making samples of colors. During the day the workers applied the color, following my instructions. Each specialized worker put on only one color. The total often exceeded twenty."
     Elizabeth Thuillier
     film colorist

gray. The film was handed over to workshops specializing in tinting photographic proofs and slides for the magic lantern. The dyes could be mixed before application or right on the film. Variations in the dilution of the dyes or in the execution of the work meant that each hand-tinted film was a unique object.

After 1903–4 stencils were used to apply the colors; this technique reduced the fluctuations in tints and contours. Production houses teamed up with coloring studios employing several hundred workers, usually women, for this work. It was not until 1906 that machines would be used to cut out stencils and apply dyes—these were the first steps away from the pictorialism of the 19th century.

Research in color photography inspired the first attempts at color filmmaking (opposite and left, various early examples). In 1899 the Englishmen Edward R. Turner and F. Marshall Lee recorded the images for a film through three separate filters—red, blue, and green—and then projected them at the same time by means of a projector with a triple lens. In 1906 the director George Albert Smith obtained a patent for Kinemacolor, a two-color process based on Charles Urban's Bioscope; it was the first color process to be marketed commercially. Both camera and projector functioned at thirty-two frames per second—twice the usual speed—and the filming was done through a rotating wheel with red and green filters. This two-color system would be widely used in many countries from 1908 into the 1920s.

Finally, mechanical monochrome processes were developed; they were cheaper and complemented these artisanal methods. Toning, which consisted of replacing the metallic silver of the image with a colored organic salt, affected only the darker parts, whereas monotinting colored the entire film. The effects obtained were more limited than could be achieved with hand tinting and were governed by stylistic conventions: Blue signified night; yellow, the sun; green, exteriors; and red, a fire or a sunset.

Edison on the Path to the Talkies

A diaphragm mounted with a steel needle recording sound vibrations in the grooves on a cylinder—such was the phonograph Thomas Alva Edison invented in 1878. It was eleven years before the apparatus attained a quality sufficient for it to be exploited commercially.

Edison conceived of his Kinetoscope as an optical counterpart to the phonograph, and even though he was forced to abandon this first version of the apparatus, the reproduction of images remained forever linked, in his mind, to that of sound. Certain scenes were recorded simultaneously for the phonograph and Kinetoscope, the thinking being that the same installations might offer the public both new attractions. The repertoire of the cylinders would remain a source of inspiration for the early cinema.

The Kinetophone, a device that combined "Edison's two marvels," stimulated the research of the Frenchman Auguste Baron who, in 1896, patented a "system serving to record and reproduce simultaneously both visual scenes and sound." It was truly synchronized: Microphones installed above the set were connected

In his studio (below) Auguste Baron set out a complete project for "100 percent talking" film, consisting of theatrical scenes, songs, and circus and music hall acts, recorded on strips 50 mm wide. But his system was too complicated to be marketed commercially. Above: A poster for the Biophonographe.

to a separate sound booth where the transmitted vibrations were engraved in copper. A single motor drove the camera and the phonograph simultaneously and at the same speed. In 1898 Baron, with the help of Félix Mesguich, set up a studio in which he shot four-minute-long films of people singing. But he would soon abandon his work.

Even if Synchronizing the Phonographic Cylinder with the Film Was Hardly Successful, the Experiments in Talking Pictures Carried On

In a small booth of the Universal Exposition of 1900, at the "Phono-Cinéma-Théâtre," one could see and hear Sarah Bernhardt declaim *Hamlet.* Clément Maurice, who had been a cameraman with the Lumière brothers, had teamed up with a phonograph manufacturer, Henri Lioret. The actors were filmed and then recorded separately; during projection, the operator turned his crank to the rhythm of what he heard in his ear trumpet.

The repertoire was high toned: In addition to Sarah Bernhardt, various well-known actors and dancers all agreed to appear before the camera. In the swarm of the exposition, the Phono-Cinéma-Théâtre scarcely

Punch's Almanac for 1879 prefigured the inventions to come by imagining that, thanks to Edison, grandparents would be able to be in contact with their grandchildren by long-distance sound and "electrical images."

While the principle of the phonograph won admiration, its sound distortion disappointed those who heard it.

attracted any interest, but its half-failure did not dissuade Clément Maurice from undertaking a European tour the following year. Two other talking cinemas, the Théâtroscope and the Phonorama, were tried out at the turn of the century. For the latter, Félix Mesguich resisted filming the theater, but instead directed cinematographic "cries of Paris," scenes of daily life in the French capital.

At this time, no one had a solution to the problem of meshing the visual and the sound recordings. On the one hand, phonographs were neither sufficiently sensitive in recording—the actors had to station themselves very close to the phonographic horns, which were therefore visible in the shot—nor were they powerful enough for reconstituting the sound. And on the other hand, the synchronization of the phonograph and the projector during projection was still very rough.

Films with sound were one of the great concerns of the French producer Léon Gaumont. In 1902 he demonstrated some trials to the scientific world; they caused a sensation. He had his actors record their text and then, in front of the camera, perform gestures and move their lips in time to what had been engraved on the cylinder. In the cinemas the motor of the Chrono-photographe was driven by the motor of the phonograph, so the two were in close alliance. Numerous "phonoscènes" were thus created and regularly appeared on the movie-house programs.

Other processes combining the phonograph and the motion picture were developed by various inventors, including Gaumont, with his Chronophone, and Oskar Messter in Germany. Choosing a new path, Frenchman Henri Joly experimented with the recording of sound on the image track itself. But he lacked the means to pursue his research, whereas another Frenchman, working in the United States, Eugène Lauste, conceived a

Before becoming interested in the talking cinema, Oskar Messter, manufacturer of optical devices, constructed Kinema-tographs (below), established the first Kino in Berlin, and launched himself into production.

"Apart from the very real and delicate pleasure one feels at this spectacle, one cannot help having the agreeable and consoling thought that here are fine gestures being recorded for eternity and that, if people of our generation know [the actors] Talma and Rachel by hearsay, our great-nephews will admire the sublime attitudes of Sarah, will hear the clarion voice of Coquelin and will relive our emotions and our artistic joys. Is that not the realization of a fine dream? We should be glad to live in an era when such chimeras become realities."

Le Figaro
8 June 1900

Above: Edison's first tries at making a talking picture.

Below: Poster advertising the Gaumont chronomegaphone.

CHRONOMÉGAPHONE. L. GAUMONT & Cⁱᵉ

system for the optical recording of sound, fixed not on a cylinder but on a narrow band alongside the image.

Sound Tables, Orchestras, and Lecturers to the Rescue of Silent Images

The idea of imitating sounds was borrowed from the theater. The sound person was placed behind the movie screen with various materials gathered on a "sound table," and he accompanied the projection. With the right materials—and a little bit of imagination—he was able to convey almost any relevant sound. He poured rice onto a zinc tray to imitate hail, shook sheet metal to render the rumbling of thunder, rubbed metallic brushes or stirred dry peas when waves broke, blew into the glass chimney of a lantern when a lion roared, and so forth. All the phases of a train's motion—the departing whistle, jets of steam, acceleration, and braking—were accompanied by their respective sound effects.

Ever since the first shows at the Grand Café, a piano had accompanied the projection in order to cover the sound of the projector and to emphasize the emotional effects of the film. When a film was being shown in a regular theater, a music hall, or a café-concert, the establishment's pianist was pressed into service to support the spectacle and fill the

Sheet metal could be used very effectively to simulate thunder. "The setup is simple, inexpensive, and it gives satisfactory results, on condition that the metallic sheet is not too skimpy so that its sound is sour and shrill," said one manual.

interludes. The first movie orchestras, however, were stationed outside the hall, with the aim of attracting customers. Inside, most cinema musicians improvised or, more often, quoted well-known tunes, fashionable songs, and snippets from classical works. The score that Gaston Paulin wrote to accompany Emile Reynaud's "Luminous Pantomimes" presented in Paris starting in 1892 may be considered to be the ancestor of original film music.

The cinema adopted the magic-lantern show tradition of having a lecturer, who both animated the show and ensured that its subject would be understood. This colorful craft disappeared with the growth of intertitles, printed messages that first announced the name of the film and the production house (the names of the director, actors, and technicians would long remain anonymous) and later were inserted into the body of the film to announce the topic of a particular sequence or to point out a digression.

The sound and musical accompaniment—as important as they may seem from this perspective—was nevertheless not always present.

In fact, some viewers were taken with the muteness of the images. Writer Louis-Ferdinand Céline later remembered his feelings in 1901 at the age of seven: "We stayed for three shows in a row. It was the same price, one franc for every seat, 100 percent silent, without sentences, without music, without captions, just the whir of the machine. You came back...."

Fairground booths were among the first cinemas, which boasted very elaborate décor, inspired by art nouveau and often emphasized by abundant lighting. The pride of the establishment, an organ in painted and sculpted wood, was placed beside the cash register. The barker helped attract spectators.

Topical films, historical tableaux, comedies, dramas, fantasies, trick scenes, risqué scenes, and religious pageants—motion pictures were soon divided into strict genres. However, the youthfulness of the new art allowed imaginative spirits to experiment with many innovations.

CHAPTER III
EARLY MASTERS

The magic function of animated pictures endured, from a Phenakistoscope disk (right) to the phantoms escaping from the *Chaudron Infernal* (*Infernal Cauldron*, opposite) of Georges Méliès.

For a Century, Special Effects in Light Projections Had Been Perfected for Purposes of Magic, Entertainment, or Instruction

The magic lantern was, first and foremost, a drawing-room entertainment. But the development of powerful artificial light sources brought it to the theatrical stage, where, in conjunction with mirrors and revolving magnifying lenses, it became increasingly effective and enjoyed ever-growing popularity. Meanwhile, people discovered the educational impact of a projected image, and the magic lantern became associated with a movement for popular education during the second half of the 19th century. The projectors, which could possess several lenses, became particularly sophisticated, reconstructing movement, and allowing one image to metamorphose or dissolve into the next.

Magicians, Quick to Promote Cinema, Conspired in What Ended Up Becoming the Ruin of Their Own Art

Magic shows—with their projections, automatons, and creative uses of electricity—foreshadowed the cinematographic spectacle, as the link between magic and the cinema grew closer at the end of the century. The Robert-Houdin Theater in Paris and the Egyptian

The silhouettes of three well-known figures of the day from Félicien Trewey's repertoire.

Italian illusionist Leopoldo Fregoli was one of the first to whom the Lumière brothers agreed to sell a camera. He filmed himself performing his acts and sold the films (poster, far left).

Röntgen rays, or X rays, would quickly cease being a source of curiosity (poster, left) and be used exclusively for scientific purposes.

Hall in London, the most famous of the theaters featuring magic, put "animated views" on their programs very early. A large number of magicians are among the pioneers of the cinema.

Félicien Trewey, one of the great names in illusionism, was a shadowgrapher: With his agile fingers, he created shadows imitating celebrities' silhouettes and then engaged them in comic sketches. He was a friend of Antoine Lumière's, who entrusted him with his sons' invention in England. Trewey organized the first public showings of the Cinématographe there, starting on 20 February 1896 at London's Marlborough Hall. Soon it became an established feature at the Empire Theatre. Later, after competition and commercial pressure forced him to return to his former craft, Trewey also shot some films.

The American illusionist Carl Hertz, passing through London before embarking for South Africa, procured from inventor Robert W. Paul a projector called the Theatrograph, the marvel of the day. During the sailing Hertz organized the first motion-picture show given on board ship. Even though he had learned to operate the projector in one evening, and though he had only a few films, he racked up premieres and triumphs in South Africa, Australia, Burma, and India.

The conjurer David Devant projected moving pictures on the stage of London's Egyptian Hall with Robert W. Paul's Animatograph. Paul filmed him while he performed his acts.

The Magic Lantern

The magic lantern was described as early as 1646 by German Jesuit scholar Athanasius Kircher in his treatise *Ars Magna Lucis et Umbrae*. According to an 18th-century definition, it was a "small machine that serves to make seen on a white wall diverse specters and frightful monsters so that those who do not know the secret believe that they belong to the magic arts." The scene at the upper left is of an early-19th-century magic show; below is a painted magic-lantern slide depicting the creation of the earth, a typically serious subject. Opposite: An 18th-century painting called *Magic Lantern*.

② ④

Entertainments in Light

A tradition of popular shows preceded the arrival of the cinema. In the 18th and 19th centuries, the puppet box theater was presented in the street and at fairs. By pulling strings, the showman played out scenes lit by candles (opposite). At the end of the 19th century, the magic-lantern plates were painted by hand or could be covered with chromolithographs (left) or photographs. The shadow theater was rejuvenated in cabaret shows; an image from an 1896 shadow-theater tableau called *Cleopatra* is below.

Though many magicians would find the cinema to be more of a menace than a boon, it was fashionable for them to name the gadgets they used in their acts after themselves. Thus we have Philip Anderson's Andersonoscopograph, Emile and Vincent Isola's Isolatograph, and Leopoldo Fregoli's Fregoligraph.

His Passion for Magic Led Georges Méliès to the Forefront of the Cinema

"One evening in 1931," wrote the film historian Georges Sadoul, "quitting his toy shop, Georges Méliès, old and ruined, put on his best coat to participate in a banquet set for three hundred guests. Over dessert, Louis Lumière, an industrialist and member of the Institute, gave him an accolade and hung on his chest a miniature Legion of Honor, saying: 'I salute in you the creator of the moving-picture spectacle.'"

Back in 1888 the Robert-Houdin Theater was for sale. Georges Méliès, then twenty-seven years old, purchased this centerpiece of "white magic," which still basked in the prestige of its founder, Robert Houdin, a famous 19th-century French magician. Passionate about magic and drawing, the young man created on the theater's small stage

"Georges Méliès had… the manual skill of an artisan. But he was above all an artist and a creator.… He had always lived like a grand gentleman, always holding open house, having a carriage, coachman, servants, property in Montreuil, property in Paris. He ruined himself for the cinema, while other film producers got rich. The first shop that my grandparents could obtain at the Montparnasse railway station was a kiosk in an open-air market. **"**
Madeleine
Malthête-Méliès,
granddaughter of
Georges Méliès

Méliès (below and opposite, at his shop in around 1929).

conjuring tricks and sketches combining fairy pantomime, the fantastic, illusions, and clowning. Automatons, stage machinery, sets that he painted himself, and fresh subjects soon came together in the films of this master illusionist. Starting in April 1896, Méliès projected some "animated photographs" as part of his show, using a device called the Kinetograph. He began by presenting film strips from the Edison Kinetoscope, and then moved on to films he had made himself in the Lumière style.

When He Discovered the Camera's Unsuspected Properties, Méliès Launched into Production

One day while filming the Place de l'Opéra in Paris, Méliès would later say, the film jammed in his camera. He freed it and resumed shooting. When he projected the sequence, to his great surprise he saw a bus change

Les Illusions Fantaisistes (*Whimsical Illusions,* 1909) is a vanishing act recalling the Robert-Houdin Theater style.

into a hearse, and men metamorphose into women. As a result of this incident—significant, even if apocryphal—which revealed to him the possibilities of the "trick of substitution by stopping the camera," magic and the cinema come together in the work of Georges Méliès. He applied this process for the first time in 1896 in the film *Escamotage d'une Dame Chez Robert-Houdin* (*The Vanishing Lady*), a classic magic act of the time. There was no longer any need for trapdoors, levers, or invisible wires. It sufficed to stop turning the camera crank while the lady left the scene. The process was so simple that he used more effects: A skeleton replaced a woman on a chair—stop—and she reappeared.

Enthusiastic, Georges Méliès in 1897 had constructed a "posing studio" in the garden of his villa at Montreuil-sous-Bois, a suburb of Paris. This studio boasted a huge, glass-walled warehouse containing a stage with machinery duplicating that at the Robert-Houdin

Above: A scene from *A Trip to the Moon.*

Theater. More than five hundred titles were filmed on this stage between 1896 and 1913—*Cendrillon* (*Cinderella*), *L'Homme Orchestre* (*One-Man Band*), *Barbe-Bleue* (*Bluebeard*), *L'Eruption Volcanique à la Martinique* (*The Eruption of Mount Pelée*), *Le Voyage dans la Lune* (*A Trip to the Moon*), *Le Sacre d'Edouard VII* (*The Coronation of Edward VII*), *Les Quatre Cents Farces du Diable* (*The Merry Frolics of Satan*), and more—and Méliès never ceased his activities as a magician and director of the theater.

The Creations of Méliès's Star-Film Company Were Distinguished by Their Special Effects

The "magus of Montreuil" worked in all genres, including topical, historical, drama, and comedy. But it was primarily in fairy stories inspired by the operettas and pantomimes of the Châtelet Theater, that what he himself would call the "Méliès style" would manifest itself with the greatest sparkle. The man who would later, old and forgotten, end up hawking toys at Paris's Montparnasse train station was a true creator who conceived and meticulously designed the tableaux of his films before directing them and, most often, performing in them himself.

Méliès's world was defined by an aesthetic and by certain themes, but above all by a technique founded on special effects, which he may not have invented, but which he always used with the greatest mastery. Besides the "stop-substitution,"

Opposite below: To make his head grow in *L'Homme à la Tête de Caoutchouc* (*The Man with the Rubber Head*, 1902), Méliès shut himself in a box covered with black velvet placed in front of a black background. The box moves toward the camera on an inclined rail, so that the apparently severed neck coincides with the edge of the tabletop.

Advertisements come to life and attack policemen in *Les Affiches en Goguette* (*The Hilarious Posters*, 1906).

Le Raid Paris–Monte Carlo en Deux Heures (*An Adventurous Automobile Trip*)

This film made by Méliès in 1905 was commissioned by the Folies Bergère, which explains the presence of several performers and the director of the famous Parisian music hall. In it, the king of Belgium, Léopold II, famous for his car accidents, bets that he can drive from Paris to Monte Carlo, down on the Mediterranean, in two hours, and manages to do so after many setbacks. These four stills are taken from a colored print of the time. King Léopold takes off in front of the Paris opera house, and makes a rapid descent (opposite); climbing the Alps by automobile, and the travelers in Dijon (this page).

Le Royaume des Fées
(*The Fairy Kingdom*)

Inspired by *The Sleeping Beauty* and made in 1903, *The Fairy Kingdom* is Méliès's first film longer than about one thousand feet, the equivalent of about fifteen minutes of screen time. It tells the story of the Princess Azurine, who is engaged to Prince Bel Azor in the presence of the fairies. But they have forgotten to invite the witch, who has the princess kidnapped. Bel Azor, searching for her, suffers a shipwreck and finds himself in Neptune's kingdom before he manages to kill the witch and rescue Azurine, whom he finally marries. Rare among the work of the director at this time, *The Fairy Kingdom* includes a scene shot outdoors, in the gardens of Montreuil, with a real horse.

Multiple exposures, black backdrops, and stop-motion photography were used in *Un Homme de Tête* (*The Four Troublesome Heads*, 1898), in which the theme of decapitation appears in Méliès's work for the first time.

Méliès used superimposition (multiple exposures), a process well known among photographers, which had once given rise to the fashion for "spirit pictures." He played with proportions by combining one filmed element with a second on another scale, or by bringing the subject closer to or farther away from the camera. With the precision of a magician, he used multiple superimpositions within each sequence.

In *One-Man Band* (1900) seven Georges Mélièses play seven different instruments at the same time. The dissolving slides used in magic-lantern shows inspired him to make dissolves—in which one image faded out while another faded in—linking each tableau. These different effects were realized during the shooting and were later adjusted by cuts and joins in the negative.

Even though he used such specifically cinematographic processes, Méliès did not set purely theatrical effects aside. Trapdoors, dummies, pyrotechnics, trompe l'oeil, sets with articulated parts, rails, winches, and cables were still very much part of the show.

The ninth tableau of *A Trip to the Moon* is called "Right in the Eye."

Cinematographic Art Soon Left the Méliès Style Behind, Though It Was Celebrated Worldwide

In 1902 Georges Méliès made *A Trip to the Moon*, a cocktail of the fantastic, the music hall, and the slapstick inspired by Jules Verne and H. G. Wells. This film, notable for its length and cost, found immense success in France, Great Britain, and the United States, where it was shamelessly copied.

The happiest period in the career of Georges Méliès ended four years later. Audiences' demands had begun to change. Instead of fantasy achieved with special effects and instead of a childlike imagination, they preferred comic ups and downs and realistic dramas. His conception of the cinema placed Méliès at the opposite pole from other contemporary directors: He used no close-ups but mostly wide shots; his camera was generally fixed; his editing was tied to the needs of trick shots

A Trip to the Moon, in thirty tableaux lasting thirteen minutes, made Méliès known around the world. In it, six scientists, members of the Astronomer's Club, set off for the moon in a giant mortar shell. They are taken prisoner by the Selenites and manage to escape, but their shell falls into the sea. A triumphant welcome awaits the astronomers when they are fished out by a steamship.

rather than to narrative imperatives; and he had a predilection for studio shooting. The creator of the cinematographic spectacle remained a man of the stage. As an artist, Georges Méliès refused to make concessions to an evolution he condemned.

The Animated Film Was Born

One day Emile Reynaud—photographer, projectionist, and promoter of using projection in education before he became a science teacher—discovered a Phenakistoscope, a scientific toy consisting of a disk with slots around the edge into which drawings were placed. (Spinning the disk made the image on the drawings appear to move.) Reynaud had the idea of replacing the slots on the disk with mirrors so as to increase the luminosity. His Praxinoscope, patented in 1877, was a new stage in the great march toward the motion picture. He himself drew, with extreme delicacy, the strips of images, and organized the marketing of his device, whose success was immediate. Reynaud went further, developing a Praxinoscope theater and a projected Praxino-scope coupled with a magic lantern. His next steps led him to the threshold of the invention of

In the first frames of Emile Reynaud's *By a Cabin* (above), a swimmer jumps on the shoulders of a potbellied man. Below: A poster for Reynaud's "Luminous Pantomimes" (1892).

film: He focused on developing a long band of paper on which the images would be drawn.

In 1889 Reynaud's Théâtre Optique (Optical Theater) was ready. Its principle was that of a Praxinoscope for projection, but it used images painted on a band of unlimited length, unrolling from a spool and advancing by gears fitting into sprockets. His first three strips—*Un Bon Bock* (*A Good Beer*), *Le Clown et ses Chiens* (*The Clown and His Dogs*), and *Pauvre Pierrot* (*Poor Pierrot*)—took him three years to create. When they

On the screen of the Théâtre Optique (left), a scene from *Poor Pierrot*—a pantomime for three people lasting ten minutes whose 120-foot-long film strips include five hundred images— is played.

were shown, starting in 1892, it became clear that the Théâtre Optique was no toy for private use, but a real form of public entertainment, and it attracted crowds of viewers to the Musée Grévin in Paris, where they were displayed.

Unfortunately, these modern illuminations proved very fragile. The gelatin the images were painted on cracked, the heat altered the colors, and the perforations tore. The show was interrupted for almost a year so that Reynaud could make two new strips, *Un Rêve au Coin du Feu* (*A Fireside Dream*) and *Autour d'une Cabine* (*By a Cabin*). So, months before the screenings at the Grand Café, he had designed and colored 636 images for the latter film alone.

The movement reconstructed by the Praxinoscope (above) lasted only as long as one revolution of the cylinder.

A Sad Conclusion

The end of Emile Reynaud's story is quite bitter. Faced
with two formidable competitors, the Kinetoscope and
the Cinématographe, he had to replace his elegant
drawings with filmed images retouched with color. But
the procedure he used was long and complicated, and he
managed to make only two films, *Guillaume Tell*
(*William Tell*) and *Le Premier Cigare* (*The First Cigar*)
before, in 1900, films of real events squeezed his
"Luminous Pantomimes" out of the
Musée Grévin. Some years later,
desperate, poverty-stricken, and ill, he
threw the animated strips from the Théâtre Optique into
the Seine River before dying, in 1918, in a hospice.

The First Masters of the Animated Film: An American Caricaturist and a Spanish Colorist

By exposing the film frame by frame and
altering the organization of the scene between
shots, unexpected effects could be produced.
The operators who wanted to achieve these
effects soon tinkered with their cameras so
that a single image—instead of an
unwieldy eight—would be recorded for
each turn of the handle. Pioneered by
J. Stuart Blackton in 1898, this
technique was dubbed "one turn, one
picture" in the United States; the
French referred to it as the
"American movement"
until World War I.

An Englishman who
had emigrated to the
United States,
Blackton, a
journalist and
illustrator at the
*New York
Evening
World*, was
sent to

In *El Hotel Eléctrico*
(*The Electric Hotel*) by
Segundo de Chomón,
hair is brushed and shoes
are waxed without any
apparent human
intervention. The film's
date is uncertain.
Generally dated 1905, it is
possibly from

later and influenced
by a film by J. Stuart
Blackton, *The Haunted
Hotel*, which came out
in 1907.

interview the inventor of the Vitascope. Edison convinced him to come to the studio to have his portrait taken in front of the camera. Thus in 1896 the young man made his start in the cinema. Immediately smitten, he and Albert E. Smith founded a production house, Vitagraph, which rapidly became one of the most important of its era. Why not animate real objects and drawings? In 1906 Blackton took up his pencil in front of a camera for a film called *Humorous Phases of Funny Faces.* A hand draws the faces of a man and a woman on a blackboard. When the hand withdraws, the faces roll their eyes, animated with autonomous life. The hand then comes back to erase these daring personages.

Around 1902 in Barcelona, Segundo de Chomón set up the first Spanish studio for coloring films and set out to make some animations. When in 1905 Pathé (the major French film distributor and producer of cameras) invited him to come and work there, he built a camera especially adapted for trick effects. He set the camera up

With *Humorous Phases of Funny Faces* (above), the first cartoon done in the single-frame method, Blackton linked visual effects without organizing them into a story.

A parody of the early scientific films, *Le Déjeuner du Savant* (*The Scientist's Lunch*, 1905) alternates shots of a man in his laboratory and microscopic close-ups of his lunch. *Opération Chirurgicale* (*Surgical Operation*, opposite below) recalls Doyen's films.

on scaffolding in a glass studio, which allowed him to film directly over drawings placed on the studio floor—the rostrum camera for stills sequences was born. His animated sequences demanded an enormous amount of work. Chomón's special effects were distinguished by their perfect execution, and he is now hailed as one of the ablest camera operators of his day.

Doctor Doyen's Surgical Films Revealed the Ambiguity of the Scientific Cinema

Even though it primarily gave rise to toys or fantastic images, the 19th-century research that led to the invention of the cinema was also linked to such scientific activities as studying retinal persistence of vision (the way in which the eye can retain an image even after its source has disappeared), astronomical phenomena, human and animal locomotion, and language.

A well-thought-of French surgeon, Eugène-Louis Doyen, asked Clément Maurice to film some operations in his Paris clinic. Thinking that teaching with the aid of the Cinématographe would be more effective than the "surgery on the dead" in medical schools, he hoped to make his methods known in the medical world. Once the technical difficulties of recording a long scene in a

"It is unfortunate…in this era when all social classes follow with interested curiosity, sometimes even with passion, the progress of surgery, that the nonmedical public should become more aware of it only by inadequate descriptions of what makes a good operation."
Eugène-Louis Doyen

poorly lit operating room were surmounted and the films were made, they were presented at a medical congress in Edinburgh in 1898. But French doctors objected and prevented Doyen from projecting his films at other official meetings.

In 1902 a spectacular operation by Doyen—the separation of Siamese twins, Radica and Doodica—unfolded before the camera. But, without Doyen having arranged it, the film showed up at various fairgrounds, and he discovered that his assistant cameraman had printed and sold numerous copies of his films. Doyen sued him and won. It was one of the first lawsuits to involve a movie.

Despite Doyen's experience, the cinema, following in the footsteps of magic-lantern shows, seemed ripe for scientific popularization. The camera, which could be looked at as a collective microscope, applied itself to investigating the world of the infinitely small. In studying microbes, scientific movies contributed to making the close-up a significant element of film language.

Advertisement for a movie showing microscopic life.

Réduction de l'affiche de M. A. BARRÈRE
publiée avec l'autorisation de MM. Pathé Frères
(Imprimeries d'Art, Robert et Cie)

By making such emblems as a rooster, an eagle, a daisy, a black star, or a monogram visible on the film set, the first production companies tried to control an industry still unregulated by law. An era of meteoric rises and overnight fortunes was also one of cutthroat competition. The world market was held in only a few hands.

CHAPTER IV
AN UNTAMED INDUSTRY

Charles and Emile Pathé carry a projector and a phonograph on this poster (opposite), which bears the rooster emblem of their company. The two brothers hired Ferdinand Zecca (right, in one of his own films).

Faced with the vast variety of cameras in circulation, the Lumière company had to give up its system of franchises in 1897 and turn to selling its own camera and films. Even though its output covered all genres, from the life of Christ to the advertising film, it declined in popularity, and the company ceased producing films around 1905. Its equipment manufacture and commercial exhibition would be abandoned a few years later, and the Lumière brothers, researchers and inventors at heart, would turn to other devices.

"Conquering the World, a Scene by the Pathé Brothers, 1894–19…"

In 1894 Charles Pathé, the son of a Vincennes butcher, exhibited an Edison phonograph at a fair. Encouraged by his first profits, he opened a phonographic shop and soon offered his clientele counterfeit Kinetoscopes imported from England. Then he teamed up with a skillful engineer, Henri Joly, who built a Kinetoscope with four peepholes, as well as an apparatus for both the recording and projection of films. In 1896 the Pathé Frères company began to sell its Kinetographs.

Pathé quickly became an important businessman who controlled several factories and studios. His firm, whose full name was "Compagnie Générale de Cinématographes, Phonographes et Pellicules, Anciens Etablissements Pathé Frères," marketed the best cameras, endowed with an ingenious feed mechanism ensuring uniform motion by using a Maltese cross. In 1899 a Pathé employee, a young Corsican named Ferdinand Zecca, began to produce films, and two years later he adapted a series of tableaux using wax figures from the Musée Grévin to make *L'Histoire d'un Crime* (*Crime Story*). Heartened by its success, the next year he shot *Les Victimes d'Alcoolisme* (*The Victims of Alcoholism*). But realistic and moralistic dramas were only one aspect of the firm's proliferating production, which touched on all genres. Charles Pathé wanted to cover every subject, reach every audience, and be understood in every country—and he succeeded: The rooster, the Pathé emblem, came to dominate world cinema. In 1905 a new studio was built in Vincennes. While today we may be uncertain to which of Pathé's many employees to attribute a film, we do know of several members of the directorial team. Beside Zecca, there were Lucien Nonguet, Hatto, Lépine, and finally, Gaston Velle, a conjurer and specialist in "fairy films," who soon went off to work at an Italian studio.

Above: From *L'Etang Enchanté* (*The Enchanted Pool*).

In *A la Conquête de l'Air* (*The Conquest of the Air*), a 1901 film, the image of Zecca astride a vehicle he invented was superimposed on a view of Paris.

Léon Gaumont Left Directing to His Secretary, Who Became the First Woman Filmmaker

When he was manager of an optic and photographic equipment company, Léon Gaumont became interested in motion pictures. In 1896 he built the first Chronophotographe (conceived by Georges Démeny) with which several scenes were recorded on filmstock 60 mm wide. The following year he marketed an apparatus designed for both shooting and projecting with 35-mm film, as well as a quiet and inexpensive Gaumont Chronophotographe, which met with a considerable amount of success.

The buyers of equipment demanded films to project. Gaumont, who was more attracted to technology than fiction, entrusted the directing to his young secretary, Alice Guy. Between 1896 and 1906 the energetic "Mademoiselle Alice" would be responsible for two hundred films, starting with *La Fée aux Choux* (*The Cabbage Fairy*), which she shot in her boss's garden on the outskirts of Paris. From comedies to melodramas, all of Gaumont's production during this period— with a few rare exceptions—can be attributed to Guy. From the charming and naive playlets at the beginning of her career, she soon moved on to directing more ambitious subjects, more carefully composed and longer—three hundred actors and twenty-five sets were used in *La Vie de Christ* (*The Life of Christ*) in 1906. After that, the first woman director in the world devoted herself to the creation of talking films for the Chronophone, while Etienne Arnaud took over Gaumont production and Louis Feuillade, later the creator of serial films, supplied the scenarios.

Around a modern shooting studio—one of the largest in the world—which was built in 1905, was a veritable

Below: A 1906 view of the Gaumont studios, which the company's catalogue boasted, "will allow us to create, beside comic and genre scenes, great spectacles of ever-increasing interest, thanks to its completely modern machinery and colossal dimensions.... The floor is built to support even a troop of elephants."

Before Alice Guy made this *Life of Christ* in 1906, numerous versions of the Passion had been shot. They count among the first films of longer duration.

industrial city. Elgé productions—from L. G., the initials of its author-itarian director—were successfully exported. This, the second largest French firm, was the first to open a branch in England in 1898. Under the super-vision of Colonel A. C. Bromhead, British Gaumont launched into film production and rapidly won great autonomy.

Alice Guy rounded up friends and neighborhood children, rented some costumes, cut some cabbages out of cardboard, held a sheet in front of the garden wall...and began her career as a filmmaker with *The Cabbage Fairy*.

1

2

Early Devices

Some of the many early motion-picture cameras and projectors:

1) The English Prestwich camera, patented in 1898, used 35-mm film, and was a favorite of the Gaumont firm.

2) The Darras camera, patented in 1896, used 45-mm film and had a mechanism identical to the one conceived by Louis Aimé Augustin Le Prince in 1888.

3) The Gaumont Chronophotographe with the Démeny system—this is the 1897 model in 35 mm, used by Alice Guy and Georges Méliès, which endured for fifteen years in the Gaumont studios.

4) A combined projector and viewer for glass slides, this 35-mm apparatus made by Raoul Grimoin-Sanson is equipped with an intermittent feed mechanism based on a Maltese cross.

3

4

Versatile Machines

1) In 1896 René Bunzli and Pierre-Victor Continsouza manufactured this projector, which served as a model for Pathé's.

2) The Phosphoroscope was sold by the Deyrolle Company around 1890.

3) The British Biokam, made by Darling and Wrench, was used as camera as well as projector. Patented in 1898 and sold by the Warwick Trading Company, it used 17.5-mm-wide film with a central perforation.

4) Near the end of 1896 the engineer George William de Bets built one of the first film cameras designed for amateurs. Using 35-mm film, it served as viewer, camera, and projector.

3

4

I

2

3

4

Amateurs or Professionals

1) A device intended for amateur use, Gaumont's pocket Chronophotographe, the 1900 model with the Démeny system, used 15-mm film with a central perforation.

2) The mechanism of Pathé's 35-mm projector in effect copied the Cinématographe's.

3) The Ernemann amateur camera Kino I —this is the 1902 model—used 17.5-mm-wide film with a central perforation.

4) Edison's Universal Projecting Kinetoscope, 1903 model, used 35-mm film and recorded twelve frames per turn of the crank.

Beside Artistic Originality, What Distinguished Georges Méliès Was Financial Independence

If the Pathé and Gaumont firms were large enterprises sustained by banks and external capital, the Star-Film Company of Georges Méliès jealously guarded its autonomy. Even though his *vues composées* (composed scenes) were more expensive than his competitors' films, they enjoyed quite a following; they were most popular at fairgrounds. And the films with the black star were in demand abroad, especially in English-speaking countries. In order to defend his interests better in the American market, in 1903 Méliès established a branch office in New York under the direction of his brother Gaston.

Pathé, Gaumont, and Méliès kept a close watch on one another, and it is often hard to say who copied whom. In the Pathé and Gaumont studios, they tried to copy the "Méliès genre." Both Zecca and Méliès made a film on the volcanic eruption in Martinique, and it is difficult to say which came first. And if Gaumont's *Un Monsieur qui a Mangé du Taureau* (*A Man Who Ate a Bull*) rocked the theaters with laughter, well then a gentleman would eat a camel in Pathé's version.

By 1906 times had gotten tougher. The audience turned away from the Méliès style; faced with an incipient glutted market, the Americans began to regroup, and Pathé created his own chain of theaters. Georges Méliès was left high and dry.

The strange appearance of the studio at Montreuil-sous-Bois (below) is due to the many modifications that Méliès made. Two years after the primitive studio was built in 1897, he added a ditch under the stage, a shed into which the camera could be moved back, glass-windowed additions serving as wings, and a huge building including set storerooms (opposite). Warehouses soon went up in the vicinity, since Méliès had to store all the goods necessary for his films—balloons, trains, planes, etc.—in addition to twenty thousand costumes and accessories.

Merciless Fighters, the Edison Manufacturing Company Remained the Top American Firm Until 1909

By acquiring the patent for the first American projector, developed by Thomas Armat and Charles Francis Jenkins and by presenting it under the name of Vitascope at Koster & Bial's Music Hall in New York on 23 April 1896, Edison set himself up in the United States as the inventor of the moving picture. In 1898 he sued all the manufacturers, marketers, and producers of films for counterfeiting or for the illicit use of his patents. Many small businesses quickly succumbed. One trial followed another, building into a veritable patent war that did not end until 1908, with the creation of the Motion Picture Patents Company, a cartel of American companies that even controlled imports.

The Edison company also proved itself formidable in the quality of its production, dominated by the

In 1905 Edwin S. Porter remade the image of Coney Island, location of the New York amusement park, by filming this documentary scene at night.

What Happened on Twenty-Third Street, New York City, a 1901 Porter film, shows street life (opposite). It ends with a shot of a woman whose skirt billows up when she walks over a subway ventilation grate.

personality of Edwin S. Porter. This young American seaman began in 1896 as an itinerant projectionist before working at a New York wax museum that quickly included cinematographic screenings among its attractions.

He became a camera operator in 1900 and, shortly afterward, Edison's director of production. He directed two films—*The Life of an American Fireman* (1902) and *The Great Train Robbery* (1903)—that film historians consider to be decisive in the evolution of cinemato-graphic language. After the considerable success of *The Great Train Robbery*, Porter was forced to increase his output. Especially passionate about cinema tech-nology, he experimented in some of his films with basic technical innovations, but did not use them in all his work.

Of Edwin S. Porter (above), *Moving Picture World* said, "He is the absolute master of his art, from A to Z. Here is no doubt the best qualified man that there has ever been to assume responsibility for a film studio."

The American Mutoscope and Biograph Company Was the Most Dangerous Rival of the Edison Company

William Kennedy Laurie Dickson, Edison's assistant whose name remains attached to the creation of the Kinetoscope and the first film strips, soon left Edison to participate in the founding of a rival firm. In 1895 he joined Elias Koopman, Harry Marvin, and Herman Casler to work on the development of an apparatus that was

able to compete with the Kinetoscope. Their product, the flip-card Mutoscope, allowed one to see a series of photographs in quick succession. In order to record the images, they built a camera (the Mutograph), which they differentiated as much as possible from Edison's to avoid a lawsuit.

Starting in April 1896, in a revolving open-air studio on the roof of a New York building, the American Mutoscope and Biograph Company made films using a cumbersome but exceptionally fine camera called the Biograph. Johann Gotlob Wilhelm ("Billy") Bitzer, a young electrician, was hired to operate it; later, in 1908, he would become the faithful assistant of director David Wark (D. W.) Griffith, the genius of early narrative cinema. The Biograph Company stood out by making slightly erotic films, one of the important genres in the first years of the motion picture.

The image wheel of the Mutoscope flipped through cards automatically when the hand crank was turned. The device's long-lasting popularity at amusement parks meant that it could still be found on the eve of World War II.

Opposite: To record the 1899 boxing match between Jim Jeffries and Tom Sharkey, for which it had exclusive rights, American Biograph built an imposing scaffold in the arena. The powerful spotlights necessary for shooting in the hall gave off such heat that the boxers had to take cover behind umbrellas between rounds.

In *Pull Down the Curtains, Suzie*, a one-shot film produced for Mutoscope in 1904, a man watches a woman undress. As the title suggests, the scene ends when she lowers the curtain before removing her undergarments.

In England, Small Production Houses Developed Quality Cinema

When Robert W. Paul discovered that no patent protected Edison's Kinetoscope in England, he quickly began to manufacture and sell forgeries. Not being able to procure Edison films, he hired a photographer, Birt Acres, to built him a camera. The two men shot their first films in the spring of 1895, and thus laid the basis for the British cinematographic industry. Paul's Animatograph Limited, which sold a projector called the Theatrograph or the Animatograph, focused, like many other firms of the era, on both marketing and production. Aided in the making of films by the prestidigitator Walter R. Booth, Paul specialized in fiction, using trick shots and original methods, traces of which would crop up in the work of Georges Méliès.

An American named Charles Urban arrived in London as the

representative of Maguire and Baucus, Edison's English agents. He transformed his office into an active company in its own right— the Warwick Trading Company— before founding his own production house—the Charles Urban Trading Company—in 1902. One of the first modern producers, he was an energetic businessman and talent scout.

In 1900 he hired George Albert Smith, a Brighton

In *The Motorist* (1905) a car drives around one of Saturn's rings.

Once he became the head of the Charles Urban Trading Company, Urban (left) distributed the films of Smith, Williamson, Méliès, and Lumière, and produced documentaries in his own name. His slogan was "We put the world before you."

photographer who back in 1896 had fabricated a camera and begun to make films. Urban also called on Cecil Hepworth, who soon left to found his own company in Walton-on-Thames. We owe to him one of the major films of the period, *Rescued by Rover* (1905), a fluidly told account of a dog saving an infant.

An interest in the magic lantern pushed a Brighton pharmacist, James A. Williamson, to follow his friend George Albert Smith. He made a camera around 1897, and the films he shot sold well. His productions, more important from a formal than an economic point of view, ended in 1909, and he would sell his Brighton studio to Charles Urban the next year.

Despite its exceptional narrative quality and the fundamental influence it exercised on directors of the period, English production played only a modest role in the international film market.

In making *Upside Down; or The Human Flies*, Booth and Paul used upside-down sets to produce the effect below.

In 1898, convinced that it was possible to live off the cinema, James A. Williamson abandoned his job as a pharmacist to devote himself exclusively to film production, at which he flourished for several years. He engaged in much export, principally to the United States and Germany. These photographs, taken in his Brighton studios, are rare glimpses of the different phases in the making of a film (left to right, from opposite above): the development of the negative, the drying, the printing of copies, and the inspection of films on a winding machine.

Cameras soon began to record actual events, participating in the new concept of information brought about by the rise of photography and the illustrated press. While sporting events, military parades, and international conflicts were the favorite subjects of newsreel films, by recording people coming out of theaters or shopping at street markets, the movies were also the mirror of everyday life.

CHAPTER V
THE DISCOVERY OF THE WORLD

Heroism distinguished the first film reporters, such as Joseph Rosenthal (opposite). But topical films were not always authentic, like *The Eruption of Mount Pelée* (right), created in the studio by Georges Méliès.

Two Kinds of Topical Film—Authentic and Staged—Coexisted During the First Decade of the Motion Picture

The explosion of the American battleship *Maine* in Havana harbor in 1898 triggered the Spanish-American War. Cameramen rushed to Cuba. Rebuffed by the American military command, they retreated to the New York City suburbs to film battles they re-created with the help of painted backdrops, basins of water, and models of ships. This is an early example of a characteristic method of reconstructing large-scale scenes in the studio.

If faked films were sometimes presented as true, or if the actual origin of a film was left ambiguous, it was not always a case of deception. In fact, some films were proudly offered as reconstructions and appreciated as such. Certain studios, such as Georges Méliès's, began to specialize in this genre. Filmmakers made recourse to sham not just when the fleetingness or remoteness of an event, censorship by public authorities, or high cost prevented location shooting—but also in order to give more prominence to factual clarity and the impact of the spectacle.

The Reconstructions of the Dreyfus Affair Provoked the First Instance of Film Censorship

The Dreyfus Affair—the case of an 1894 espionage charge brought against a Jewish officer in the French Army who (as it turned out after he was sent to a penal colony) had been framed— mobilized French opinion and attract- ed international attention for many years.

The Dreyfus Affair inspired filmmakers from Zecca (below) to Méliès—whose sympathy spurred him not only to make the movie but to play the role of Dreyfus's defense attorney (opposite below).

While the goal of the topical cinema was to approach the event itself as closely as possible, Georges Méliès went even further in his *Le Sacre d'Edouard VII* (*The Coronation of Edward VII*): He reconstructed the ceremony before it had taken place, and was thus in a position to present his film in the theaters on the very evening the event occurred, 9 August 1902. English producer Charles Urban had requested that Méliès create this meticulous reconstruction of the coronation scene in Westminster Cathedral, which was later inserted between real shots of the arrival and departure of the royal carriage.

So it was inevitable that the affair would be filmed. When in 1898 Francis Doublier, the Lumière company's representative, met with the Jewish communities of southern Russia, everyone brought up the unfortunate Captain Dreyfus. To respond to and cash in on their expectations, the cameraman rummaged through his stock of films and cut, pasted, and transformed four bland scenes into the first film of the affair. Backed by a vibrant commentary, the movie was met with great enthusiasm, though it had to be taken off the market when it aroused the suspicion of an informed spectator.

The Boer War, pitting the Boers against the British, from 1899 to 1902, attracted to South Africa intrepid reporters like Joseph Rosenthal (below). This conflict proved particularly deadly for war correspondents: According to a newspaper report of the day, a third of them were wounded or killed. Left: A scene from Rosenthal's coverage.

During Dreyfus's appeal trial in 1899, the cameramen hoping for some real-life footage used all their craftiness and patience—but captured nothing but the gray and distant silhouette of a beleaguered man walking, hunched over, in a prison courtyard. It is easy to see, then, why Georges Méliès undertook a reconstruction of the whole affair in twelve scenes. In its exceptional length—fifteen minutes—and style—a realism directly inspired by press accounts—the film stands out from the rest of Méliès's work.

At the same time, Pathé

issued another version of the Dreyfus Affair.

The two films caused an uproar, attracting the attention of the police and alerting the censors. Ultimately, the government forbade the making and projection of any film on the subject. This measure, an unexpected legacy of the first years of the cinema, would not be lifted until 1950.

L umière films like *Les Coolies dans les Rues de Saïgon* (*Coolies in the Saigon Streets*) were shot by young people who had never traveled previously and had no journalistic training. The fresh look that they cast on the world led them to record scenes that would no doubt have been ignored by news professionals.

Camera Operator: A New Profession and a Modern Form of Adventure

Poorly defined, jobs in film were often ephemeral or done on the side, as moonlighting. If the case of Georges Méliès—at once producer, writer of scenarios, director, set designer, and actor—is extreme, one person's combining of several functions was not rare.

Pioneers in a new world, camera operators played a fundamental role—they captured images, to be sure, but they also served as founders of national film industries by establishing the bases for commercialization, production, and distribution. Many have remained unknown. Some took up this young career by chance, quitting it, like most of the Lumière cameramen, when their contracts came to an end.

Others, already professional dealers in information, like journalists or photographers, approached their craft

M ovie programs were always heterogeneous. Here, the fact-based film is followed by *Cendrillon* (*Cinderella*).

differently, employing this new technology to best advantage.

The first true film reporter, Joseph Rosenthal, was not a journalist, but a photographic technician working in London for motion-picture entrepreneur Charles Urban. When the Warwick Trading Company sent him to South Africa in 1900 to follow the British troops fighting the Boers, he traveled with two cameras and two mules. Approaching very close to the combat, he shot more than fifteen thousand feet of film.

Unfortunately, it did not all make it back to London: Some of it was stopped by the censors, and other pieces disappeared en route when a convoy was captured by the enemy or when a boat sank. The old era of battles between ranged ranks of massive troops was fading away, and with no long-range lenses to use, Rosenthal's films showed that guerrilla fighting did not look good on film, and European and American reconstructions soon appeared in the movie houses to compete with his authentic war films. Enjoying great renown, Rosenthal would follow all the great world conflicts at the beginning of the century—in China, the Philippines, and Japan.

The Cinéorama, a Circular Cinema, Tried to Simulate the Experience of a Balloon Trip

The name of Raoul Grimoin-Sanson will be recorded in film history not for the Phototachygraph (even if it was one of the Cinématographe's first competitors), but rather for a device called the Cinécosmorama, based on which he built a novel form of entertainment, the Cinéorama. This celebrated attraction never really got off the ground, so to speak, and in retrospect it was more of a utopian idea than a reality.

The Cinécosmorama, patented by the inventor in 1897, was an apparatus formed by ten radiating cameras, which permitted filming and projection in 360 degrees. More than anything, the device evoked the concept of the panorama and the

From *Un Drame dans les Airs* (*Drama in the Air,* 1904).

idea of a voyage, much in the spirit of the time.

Grimoin-Sanson conceived of a vast circular building more than three hundred feet in circumference, whose white walls served as a continuous screen. The center of the hall was occupied by an immense balloon gondola equipped with the usual accessories—anchor, rigging, sacks of ballast, and a ladder. The ceiling was covered with a hanging designed to imitate the balloon itself, with its tackle, ties, ropes, and valve opening. The ten synchronized cameras were placed under the gondola and, when the lights were dimmed, would project views of balloon ascents, voyages, and landings (the latter achieved by running the film backward).

This project was approved by the commissioners of the Paris Universal Exposition of 1900 and Grimoin-Sanson undertook to bring it to life. He had the cameras built and then shot the film footage on board real balloons soaring above the capitals of Europe. But technical imperfections ruined this grandiose enterprise: The heat thrown off by the projectors was unpleasant

Above: The Cinéorama balloon in Paris, 1900.

On a track in Pennsylvania in 1896, Edison cameramen and railroad agents at work on *Black Diamond Express*. Fiction films frequently integrated different types of train footage, offering the spectator alternately the points of view of a conductor, a passenger, and a cow watching the train go by.

for the spectators and created a fire risk, so the police ordered the establishment closed after only four performances.

An experiment without a successor, the Cinéorama seems more an ultrasophisticated avatar of the dioramas so popular in the 19th century than a prefiguring of the complete visual experience the cinema would try to become in the 20th.

The Train and the Motion Picture Were an Inevitable Combination at the Turn of the Century

"Suddenly, you hear something click; everything disappears, and a train occupies the screen. It heads straight for us—watch out! You could say that it wants to bear down into the dark where we are, to make of us an unspeakable heap of torn flesh and broken bones, and reduce to dust this hall and the whole edifice filled with wine, music, women, and vice."

This apocalyptic vision in which the filmed train, in an instant, appears as the avenger who strikes a depraved society belongs to Russian writer Maksim Gorky. The "primitive scene" of the film—the arrival of a train at a station—is a recurrent theme in the early days of the cinema. Locomotives stopped bursting through screens when cameramen, often followed by spectators, set up shop in railroad cars. The first lateral traveling shots—shots in which the camera moves, which were called panoramas at the time—were taken through train doors. The most intrepid of cameramen crouched on the front of engines and filmed the passing landscape, as it was swallowed up by speed. Train and cinema were thus combined, and this association contributed to the rise of the American motion picture industry.

Some of Hale's Tours were commissioned by railroad companies. Thus, in 1898, in Orange, New Jersey, cameraman Billy Bitzer shot an advertising film for a railroad company with a Mutograph camera attached to the cowcatcher of a locomotive.

The "Train Cinema"

Fire chief of Kansas City for more than twenty years, George C. Hale was endowed with an undeniable knack for business. In 1904 he bought the patent for an invention of William J. Keefe's consisting of a train car running on circular tracks through a tunnel; the tunnel's translucent sides served as a screen upon which films of landscapes were projected. Hale simplified Keefe's invention: His train car didn't actually move—instead its front was replaced with a film screen, and a gadget underneath simulated the rattles and sounds of a moving train. The "train cinema" was one of the novelties exhibited at the great St. Louis World's Fair in 1904, along with the ice cream cone, the hot dog, and iced tea.

The Spectacle Known as Hale's Tour Was the Basis of an American Industry

Beginning in 1905, the attraction, baptized Hale's Tour, spread across the United States, making the fortunes of its promoters—including, among others, Sam Warner, Adolph Zukor, and Carl Laemmle, who would figure among the greatest Hollywood producers some years

Scenes of trains arriving in the station were very popular in the first years of the cinema. In this one the man running in front adds a narrative dimension and fresh emotional tone to the film.

Newspapers reported that spectators watching the projection of a Hale's Tour called out to pedestrians appearing on the screen so that they would get out of the way. One man came back to the screenings every day, hoping to witness a derailment.

later. Zukor, the future president of Paramount Pictures, opened the first New York Hale's Tour in a building resembling a train station, staffed by employees in uniform who ushered the spectators into a hall seating sixty, for a half-hour trip. Five-cent Hale's Tours flourished across the country, particularly in amusement parks, forming the first permanent chain of movie theaters.

The illusion, reinforced by the opening shots of rails streaming under the train, was convincing. In fact, travel films shot from the front of moving vehicles soon became an established genre listed in the catalogues of most American production companies. Cameras explored every country in the world, for the exhibitors were always wary of monotony and strove to find the new and the exciting. But monotony inevitably did set in, and by around 1912 Hale's Tours had disappeared.

In an attempt to overcome public disaffection, Adolph Zukor inserted a successful fiction film, *The Great Train Robbery* (1903), directed by Edwin S. Porter, into his show. This landmark film marked another fundamental conjunction of train and early film and was one of the keys to the evolution of motion-picture language.

After 1905 Hale's Tours were transformed into nickelodeons, whose name linked the five-cent coin and the Odeon, the Greek word for theater.

"The hall was about fifty feet deep and the seats were on the two sides with a central aisle, exactly as in a railroad car, with the same type of cane-backed seats. The film had been taken from a train crossing the Andes. I stayed there with a friend, another kid, and for us it was like a fairy tale. We spent the whole day watching this spectacle and did not get back to earth until they threw us out in order to clean up."

Byron Askin
American director

"The public has seen too many trains, trams, and autobuses. And with the exception of a few films whose humor is too French to please the British, one could say that no one up to now has begun to exploit the possibilities of moving pictures, to make us laugh, cry, or be amazed."

Robert W. Paul, 1898

CHAPTER VI
IMAGES RUNNING WILD

This kiss, no doubt the first one in movie history, is the sole and entire subject of the film *The May Irwin–John C. Rice Kiss*, not the climax of a romantic story.

The Magic Lantern Lies at the Heart of Film Narration

The composition and aesthetic of early films trace their roots back to several narrative forms popular at the end of the 19th century, among them the magic lantern and the comic strip.

The magic lantern, which furnished the cinema with some of its first artisans, also offered a repertoire of subjects and suggested a mode of telling a story in a sequence of tableaux. Its influence was felt particularly strongly by British directors: James Williamson and George A. Smith regularly organized magic-lantern projections, and Cecil Hepworth was the son of a famous projectionist and author of a reference manual on the subject.

A series of magic-lantern slides often culminated in a shot taken from up close—in it one can see the antecedent of the concluding close-up in the cinema. The lecturer's commentary in magic-lantern shows influenced films by making it clear that certain elements did not need to be made explicit in the images themselves but could be revealed in sound during their projection.

The Impact of the Comic Strip

The fierce competition being waged between the New York press magnates Joseph Pulitzer, owner of the New York *World*, and William Randolph Hearst, owner of the *Morning Journal*, encouraged the American comic strip, which flourished, in color, on the first page of the Sunday supplements of both dailies. The comics supplied the movies with ideas for scenarios and characters, and bad boys from the school of Buster Brown or the Katzenjammer Kids abounded on the screen. Happy Hooligan, the hero of the first comic strip drawn by Frederick Burr Opper in 1899, turned up the following year in a series of films, while *The Dream of a Rarebit Fiend* by Winsor McCay inspired a film of the same name by Edwin S. Porter in 1906.

The structure of the comic strip also had an influence on the emergence of film's language: Full-page features

In Edwin S. Porter's *The Dream of a Rarebit Fiend*, a man staggers home and gets into bed, having overindulged in beer and cheese fondue. He has a nightmare—his bed shakes, rushes out of the bedroom, and flies over New York. The man falls out of bed and finds himself hanging on the steeple of a church before waking up on the ground, in his bedroom. The film is linked to the comic strip of the same title by Winsor McCay by its effects: Drunkenness is expressed by a shot of the actor clinging to a lamppost filmed by a moving camera, superimposed on a rapid horizontal panorama of the landscape. As well as superimposition, Porter's bag of tricks included frame-by-frame shooting, the horizontal division of the screen, a reduction in size of the characters, and the combination of shots of several scales.

were divided into panels equivalent to film shots which furthered the story while varying the viewing angle, scale, and location. Several comic strips, like *Buster Brown* or *Little Nemo*, began with full-page drawings that introduced the story but were not a real part of it. This initial image can be compared to the close-up with which many films opened. But, all parallels aside, in the first years of the century, film directors were far from attaining cartoonists' narrative virtuosity.

Vaudeville Had a Great Influence on the Nascent Cinema

When Dickson shot the first Kinetoscope films, he borrowed scenes from New York music halls and traveling theater troupes. In some of his films, the sets resembled theater backdrops; the artist came on stage, saluted, performed his or her number, and exited; and the camera had the best seat in the house, in the center at a middle distance. Filmed variety acts, which generally consisted of a single shot, were screened in music halls, in the spirit of the original.

Framing and Depth of Field

Directors learned very early on how to play with these elements. In fact, Lumière's *The Arrival of a Train at a Station* offers one of the oldest and most striking examples of the change of scale within a single shot. Lumière's films are remarkable in that he employed traditional standards of composition; his films are framed like photographs.

In James Williamson's *The Big Swallow* (1901), a gentleman who is reading discovers an amateur photographer who has his head under the camera's black cloth and is already in the process of taking his photograph. The gentleman orders him to leave, and comes closer and closer, gesticulating and shouting, until his head occupies the whole frame. Finally his mouth alone fills the entire screen. He opens it, and first the camera, then the photographer, disappear inside. He walks away chewing and expressing the greatest satisfaction.

Though wide-angle scenes in a frame inspired by the theatrical stage were predominant, directors did employ closer framings and variations in scale. The movements of actors—who entered and exited at the back or at the sides of the field—were borrowed from theatrical stagecraft.

Close shots—which include only the head and shoulders of an actor—or close-ups—which reveal only a hand or face—were not uncommon. They ranged from the face of Georges Démeny mouthing "*Je vous aime*" ("I love you") in front of the Chronophotographe in 1891, to *Record of a Sneeze* for the Kinetoscope in 1894, or the kiss of two actors (*The May Irwin–John C. Rice Kiss*) for the Vitascope in 1896. In fact, such shots even constituted a genre, one of whose favorite subjects was the play of facial expression, particularly grimaces. Close shots, generally showing the principal actor, could be placed either at the opening or closing of a film; in fact, *The Great Train Robbery* was delivered to exhibitors with a shot of the chief bandit firing his gun right out at the spectators; it could be placed at the exhibitor's discretion. Another frequent finale was an apotheosis in the form of a tableau vivant, a set of frozen poses.

In *The Big Swallow*, the man advances toward the camera, which remains immobile. The cameraman had to modify the focus constantly so that the image stayed sharp. *Concours de Grimaces (The Grimace Competition*, below), by Ferdinand Zecca, is a series of close-ups of faces with no narrative link.

In *La Peine du Talion* (*Tit for Tat*, 1906), the view of the entomologist with a pin through his middle, filmed with an overhead camera, is followed by a full shot of the butterflies having their revenge.

The Camera Moves: Traveling Shots and Panoramas Enlarge the Scenic Space

Other innovations involved the position of the camera. While it was generally placed at the actors' eye level, filmmakers found that it could be raised or lowered to achieve certain effects. Some trick effects were obtained by placing the camera overhead, directly above the scene.

But, at first, the camera did not budge. While Lumière's films demonstrate a remarkable expertise in framing and the use of depth of field, they consist of a single static shot. Therefore, in 1897, when cameraman Eugène Promio filmed the palaces of the Grand Canal in Venice from a moving gondola, he claimed to have made the first traveling shot in the history of the cinema.

Grouped in film catalogues under the rubric "panoramas," traveling shots, whether forward, backward, or side to side, and whether taken from a train, boat, balloon, automobile, or elevator, proliferated in documentary films well before 1900. They soon made their way into fiction films, though they were rarely used unless they could be justified or explained by the plot involving some means of locomotion.

In *L'Ingénieuse Soubrette* (*Magic Picture Hanging*, 1902) Zecca not only filmed from overhead, but he placed the wall decoration in such a way that one has the impression that the maid is walking up the wall to hang the pictures. She beckons several times to the viewer, explaining in gestures what she is going to do, and then she thumbs her nose. The practice of addressing the camera would become taboo before too long, since it destroyed the illusion of the autonomy of the cinematographic world.

In many cases characters moved from the background up to a stationary camera. *Hooligan in Jail*, produced by the American Mutoscope and Biograph Company in 1903, offered a daring example of a forward traveling shot, starting with a view of the whole cell, and moving to a close shot of the vagabond eating his prison hash. This was an innovative way to join two views, an alternative to simply cutting. But this step was not followed up: Instead of having the camera change position, Georges Méliès, adapting a theatrical device for the cinema, had his painted backdrops move instead, unrolling horizontally in front of the camera.

After 1900, when they were shooting on location, camera operators were fond of panning—pivoting— to follow a character or an action, which sometimes seems to be more a clumsy reframing of the scene than a deliberate effect. In about six years, these movements, which had by then become familiar in fiction films, had acquired a function in the story. Pans made an appearance in films made in the studio at Pathé in 1905 and would remain a characteristic of movies made by the foremost French production company for many years.

Camera movements could reveal the existence of an off-screen space where part of the action could be taking place, allowing viewers' imaginations to fill in the holes between shots.

The Chase, that Great Device of Early Cinema, Meant the Introduction of Several Innovations

The majority of fiction films were composed of a single shot. The oldest known examples of films with multiple shots are from 1898, and belong to Georges Méliès (*La Lune à un Mètre/The Astronomer's Dream*) and to Robert W. Paul (*Come Along, Do!*), which combines an interior and an exterior scene. By around 1900 films whose plots required several shots were often conceived as a series of shots, each of which bore a distinct title. Six years later films containing about ten shots and lasting ten minutes were quite common.

A policeman running after a bandit, a dog pursuing a vagabond, a grocer chasing a thief, a woman searching for her husband: The chase gave rise to longer films, consisting of several shots, made on location. Escaping studio sets, which aimed at an illusion of three-dimensionality, actors took to the streets, tumbled down stairs, forded rivers, and scaled barricades. To run more easily, women lifted their skirts, and the sight of an ankle was not the least of the attractions of the chase film, even though feminine roles were often played by cross-dressing men when acrobatics were called for.

The Moving Chase

Chase films, born in England, were quickly adopted in France and then in the United States. They shared an identical structure: Each shot was in a different location and, generally, the protagonists came out of the background, moved toward the camera, and left the shot diagonally, the camera sometimes panning to stay with them longer. The chased and the chasers thus traversed the field of vision one after another, and not until a scene was empty did the shot change. The pursuit on foot was quickly followed by chases on horseback, in automobiles, and on trains, which led to shorter shots and a faster pace.

The Motor Pirate, by Englishman Arthur Melbourne-Cooper (1906), is an early chase film. In twelve shots, the modern bandits, behind the wheel of a futurist vehicle—in fact, a disguised Panhard—attack a farmhouse and threaten its occupants. They are chased by the police, but the strange vehicle swallows one of the officers. After attacking other drivers, the bandits end up stuck in a river. The Motor Pirate seems to mock the innumerable chase scenes of the era, which were triggered by the most minor pretext and used the most varied means of locomotion. Here, the theft of chickens provokes the chase, and the plunge into the river puts an end to it.

Directors Could Convey the Complexity and Evolution of a Story Without Recourse to Editing

Simultaneous actions could be represented by juxtaposing them in the same shot, either by showing two places side by side on a painted backdrop, dividing the set with a partition, or by superimposing one image on another, completely or partially, by masking out one image and then exposing the film again. Telephone conversations were depicted by dividing the screen, showing the two interlocutors, and sometimes reserving a third of the space to convey either the content of their dialogue or simply the distance separating them. The superimposition of one image on another was used especially to represent the subjectivity of a dream, a memory, or words.

The change of place inside a shot could be indicated by a pan of the camera. In *The Little Train Robbery* (Porter, 1905), a parody of *The Great Train Robbery*, the camera follows the fleeing bandits and then pivots, coming back to their victims on the train.

Multiple shots did not always add up to a continuous story, as breaks or ellipses were numerous. *Uncle Tom's Cabin*, for example, directed by Edwin S. Porter in 1903, assumed that spectators were already familiar with Harriet Beecher Stowe's novel, since the story is so condensed and chopped up.

Superimposition helped tell a story visually. *What the Curate Really Did* (1905, left) shows a curate talking with a young girl and then in a series of superimpositions shows gossiping women distorting the story. As the film progresses from shot to shot, the little girl grows up until she finally becomes a woman whom the curate embraces.

In *The Dreyfus Affair* (opposite above), the screen is divided into three superimposed parts to depict a telephone conversation.

Zecca showed the dream of a condemned man in *Crime Story* by using a specially designed set (opposite below).

These postcard advertisements for Liebig's meat extract show how various trick shots from popular movies were filmed. Left to right, top row: *Catastrophe de Chemin de Fer* (*Railroad Disaster*) was made with miniature models. Using a film of fish swimming in an aquarium, the creators of *La Sirène* (*The Mermaid*) recorded a woman pretending to swim. *La Fuite de Potirons* (*The Pumpkins' Escape*) was created by filming pumpkins rolling down a hillside street while the man ran backward toward the cart. When the film is played backward, it appears that the pumpkins flee up the street. The car in *L'Accident d'Automobile* (*The Automobile Accident*) was filmed running over the artificial limbs of a legless man. The camera was stopped, and an actor dressed in the same way replaced the man. The burglar climbs up the set of a facade filmed from above in *La Dextérité d'un Monte-en-l'Air* (*The Dexterity of a Cat Burglar*). Main picture: The special effect in *Rêve de Trottin* (*Dream of an Errand Girl*) was made by creating an opening in the backdrop corresponding exactly to the basket lid. The basket was opened, the camera was stopped, and the scene resumed with the girls in position.

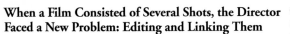

When a Film Consisted of Several Shots, the Director Faced a New Problem: Editing and Linking Them

The oldest mode of transition between shots was the dissolve, an overlap between the outgoing and incoming shots, a device first used by Georges Méliès that was quickly adopted in American and other French productions. For example, all the shots in Ferdinand Zecca's *Crime Story* (1901) and Edwin S. Porter's *The Life of an American Fireman* are joined by dissolves. Dissolves began to lose favor after 1903, and only Méliès would persist in their use.

The British introduced the use of the simple cut between two shots, done before the field of vision became empty or the action in question was carried to completion. Two films by James Williamson, *Stop Thief!* (1901) and *Fire!* (1902) thus had a completely novel feeling. In them, the action is not followed from one shot to another continuously but is partially repeated in the second shot. This specific device in the syntax of the early years of the cinema was used when there was a change of place or a change of framing of the same event.

Again, an Englishman, this time George Albert Smith, was the first to divide the same scene into several shots and insert close-ups between the wide shots. First, the

"Perhaps the film that most dramatically uses the close-up to increase the sense of both voyeurism and eroticism is *The Gay Shoe Clerk* (Edison). It changes from a long shot to a close-up of the salesman and his female customer, with a close-up of his hands tying her shoe. The film then cuts to a long shot of him kissing her. In effect, the sudden change in camera position from a long to close shot indicates, even hypostatizes, the intense erotic desire which the characters have come to feel for each other. "
John Hagan
film historian

presence of a magnifying glass, a telescope, or a keyhole would signal to the viewer that a close-up would follow; and then it would appear, the image circumscribed by a black mask around the edges of the frame, emulating the shape of the object theoretically being looked through. Shots of the characters watching something alternated with close-ups showing what they saw. After 1903 close-ups served not only to indicate the actor's point of view but also focused the attention of the spectator on a

In *A Wonderful Hair Restorer*, the shot of Zecca examining this man's bald cranium with a magnifying glass is followed by a masked close-up. This type of shot, which shows what the actor is looking at, is called a point-of-view (or subjective) shot.

detail of the scene without the intervention of optical instruments or masks.

This was a time of much variety and experimentation. Clichés had not yet developed. One method of getting from one shot to the next would be used one time, and another device would be used the next. Chase films would experiment with a variation in points of view, as

well as shot-countershot sequences, but such techniques did not catch on widely.

The Great Train Robbery, the First Western, Was One of the Great Popular Successes at the Beginning of the Century

This film reveals remarkably well how one could, after only a few years of fiction cinema, tell a story. Edwin S. Porter linked scenes one after another without dissolves, by using simple cuts that came before the dramatic action or logic of the scene was played out entirely. The basic unit of the film is not the tableau, but the shot, and the film's fourteen shots, particularly the exteriors, are dynamic.

The Great Train Robbery's success attests to the fact that a wide public was already familiar with the new artistic form and its mode of expression, to the point of enjoying, beyond technique or novelty, the potentials of emotion and suspense. In the organization of scenes showing the evil deeds of the bandits and those shots presenting the preparations of the forces of justice, one

A remarkable shot-countershot, this view of children filmed from behind throwing snowballs at the glass door of a house is followed by a shot from the front as they throw their snowballs at the camera lens (*Their First Snowballs,* 1907).

New York was the capital of American cinema, and most of the exteriors were shot in New Jersey in those days. But the sun, wide-open spaces, and natural beauty of southern California attracted film crews, and the business moved west around 1910. Opposite below: Hollywood in 1905.

can see the precursors to the way in which a few years later D. W. Griffith crosscut between multiple developing scenes to tell several stories and express the simultaneity of two or more actions.

But the cinema was still so young. Griffith, whose name would mark the beginning of a new era in movie history and stand for the art of silent film, was still a poverty-stricken young man, dreaming of being a writer, trudging from one New York production house to another in the hope of peddling a scenario or getting a bit part. And Hollywood was still a sleepy, sun-drenched valley, known only for its fruit.

Anomalies of time were customary in early cinema. When one changed the angle of vision in shooting a chase, one reshot the scene from an earlier stage. Here, in *The Little Train Robbery*, the position of the characters is repeated, one step further back, in the following shot.

DOCUMENTS

First Impressions, First Thoughts

The press proved relatively sparing in its coverage of the first screenings. These published comments only hint at the excitement that must have been felt at the time.

Messieurs Lumière, father and son, from Lyon, last evening invited the press to the inauguration of a truly strange and novel spectacle, whose premiere was reserved for the Parisian public. They have installed their ingenious apparatus in the elegant basement of the Grand Café in the Boulevard des Capucines.

Imagine, if you will, a screen placed at the back of a vast room, as large as can be imagined. This screen is visible by a crowd. On the screen appears a photographic projection. So far, nothing new. But suddenly, the image —of either natural or reduced size, depending on the scene's dimensions— animates itself and comes to life.

It is a factory gate, which opens and releases a flood of workers, male and female, with bicycles, running dogs, and carriages—all swarming and milling about. It is life itself; it is movement captured on the spot.

Or else there is an intimate scene, a family gathered around a table. Baby lets some porridge which his father is feeding him fall from its lips, while the mother smiles. In the distance, the trees are swaying; one sees the breeze lift the child's ruffle....

Photography has ceased to record immobility. It perpetuates the image of movement. The beauty of the invention resides in the novelty and ingenuity of the apparatus.

When these gadgets are in the hands of the public, when anyone can photograph the ones who are dear to them, not just in their immobile form, but with movement, action, familiar gestures, and the words out of their mouths, then death will no longer be absolute, final.

La Poste, 30 December 1895

Inspired by a famous picture story, *The Sprinkler Sprinkled* was shot by Louis Lumière in the family's vegetable garden during the summer of 1895.

A new invention by Thomas A. Edison was shown to a few favored persons last night. The new machine is really a grown up kinetoscope, and it is a success.

Mr. Edison calls his latest invention the Vitascope, which he says means a machine showing life, and that is exactly what the new apparatus does.

The vitascope, which has been in process of perfection at the Llewellyn laboratory for the last seven or eight months, under Mr. Edison's direction, is the ideal he had in mind, he says, when he began work on the kinetoscope machine, with which he has never been satisfied.

The vitascope is an improvement of the kinetoscope, by which moving life size figures of men, women and animals are thrown upon a screen by means of bright lights and powerful lenses. The trial of the new machine was made last night in a cold corner of the big foundry at the works, and Mr. Edison, with Richard N. Dyer, William J. Gilmour, manager of the phonograph work Raff & Gammon, of New York, and a few invited guests huddled around a red hot stove and gazed at and admired the marvellous figures thrown upon the big white screen at one end of the room.

The first picture shown was a colored panorama of a serpentine dance by Anabelle, who went out to West Orange to pose one day last summer. The film roll on which the photographs were attached was arranged over a half dozen spools and pulleys, and the machine was set in motion.

Even the inventor himself was surprised at the result, although with his usual critical eye he discovered flaws in the film which he declared must be disposed of before the vitascope would come up to his ideal.

New York Herald
4 April 1896

That settles scenery. Painted trees that do not move, waves that get up a few feet and stay there, everything in scenery we simulate on our stages will have to go. Now that art can make us believe that we see actual living nature, the dead things of the stage must go.

And think what can be done with this invention! For instance, [singer Albert] Chevalier comes on the screen. The audience would get all the pantomime of his coster songs. The singing, words fitted to gestures and movements, could be done from the wings or behind the curtain. And so we could have on the stage at any time any artist, dead or alive, who ever faced Mr. Edison's invention.

Charles Frohman
New York theater magnate
The New York Times
24 April 1896

Every seat in the theatre was sold ere the box office window was opened for the evening's business. Standing room only was sold, and the purchasers of it formed a fresco around the entire circuit of the walls from box to box in addition to which some hundreds who applied for seats left, to come again later in the week. So much for what was expected of the management, and it can be said but in a few words, the immense audience was not disappointed....

Los Angeles Herald
7 July 1896

The vitascope is a wonder, a marvel, an outstanding example of human ingenuity, and it had an instantaneous success on this, its first exhibition in Los Angeles.

Los Angeles Times
7 July 1896

Novelist Maksim Gorky's report took on quite a different tone.

Last evening, I was in the Kingdom of the Shadows.

If one could only convey the strangeness of this world. A world without color and sound. Everything here—the earth, water, and air, the trees, the people—everything is made of a monotone gray. Gray rays of sunlight in a gray sky, gray eyes in a gray face, leaves as gray as cinder. Not life, but the shadow of life. Not life's movement, but a sort of mute specter.

Here I must try to explain myself before the reader thinks I have gone mad or become too indulgent toward symbolism. I was at Aumont's restaurant and I saw the Lumière Cinématographe, the moving pictures. This spectacle creates an impression so complex that I doubt I am able to describe all its nuances. I will however try to convey the essentials.

When the lights are extinguished in the hall where we are to be shown the Lumière brothers' invention, a great gray image—the shadow of a poor engraving—suddenly appears on the screen; it is *A Paris Street*. Examining it, one sees carriages, buildings, people— all immobile—and you predict that the spectacle will have nothing new: views of Paris, who has not seen them so many times? And suddenly, with a curious click on the screen, the image is brought to life. The carriages that were in the background of the image come right toward you. Somewhere in the distance people appear, and the closer they get, the more they grow. In the foreground children play with a dog, bicyclists turn and pedestrians seek to cross the street. It all moves, breathes with life, and suddenly, having reached the edge of the screen, disappears one knows not where.

This is all strangely silent. Everything takes place without your hearing the noise of the wheels, the sound of footsteps or of speech. Not a sound, not a single note of the complex symphony which always accompanies the movement of a crowd. Without noise, the foliage, gray as cinder, is agitated by the wind and the gray silhouettes—of people condemned to a perpetual silence, cruelly punished by the privation of all the colors of life—these silhouettes glide in silence over the gray ground.

Their movements are full of vital energy and so rapid that you scarcely see them, but their smiles have nothing of life in them. You see their facial muscles contract but their laugh cannot be heard. A life is born before you, a life deprived of sound and the specter of color—a gray and noiseless life—a wan and cut-rate life.

It is terrible to see, this movement of shadows, nothing but shadows, the specters, these phantoms; you think of the legends in which some evil genius causes an entire town to be seized by a perpetual sleep and you think you have seen some Merlin work his sorcery in front of your eyes. He has bewitched the whole street, compressed the high buildings; from roof to foundations, they are squeezed into a space that seems to be only a meter wide; the people were shrunk proportionally at the same time as their ability to speak was stolen, and as the earth and the sky were plundered of their colored pigment and draped in the same gray monotone.

This grotesque creation is presented to us in a sort of niche at the back of a restaurant. Suddenly, you hear something click; everything disappears, and a train occupies the screen. It heads straight for us—watch out! You could say that it wants to bear down into the dark where we are, to make of us an unspeakable heap of torn flesh and broken bones, and reduce to dust this hall and the whole edifice filled with wine, music, women, and vice.

But no! It is only a cortege of shadows.

Maksim Gorky
Nijegorodskilistok
4 July 1896

This Russian poster was annotated by a French camera operator to correspond with the order of the programmed projection.

Lumière Remembers

Author Georges Sadoul took the opportunity to interview the charming Louis Lumière in 1948. The elderly man remembered much about the historic events of more than a half-century earlier.

I had not the honour of knowing the great inventor who has just died when I received from him in August, 1946, a manuscript consisting of some dozen pages entitled "Observations suggested to Louis Lumière by reading Georges Sadoul's book entitled: 'L'Invention du Cinéma.'" In this monograph he had taken the trouble to rectify certain errors in the first volume of my Histoire Générale du Cinéma, *completing my data on a number of points.*

M. Louis Lumière received me a few weeks later at Bandol. In the course of this long interview—and of those which followed—he furnished me with a large body of information concerning his cinematograph, and this enabled me to prepare a very much augmented and corrected edition of "L'Invention du Cinéma."…

Louis and Auguste Lumière photographed by their father.

In January last [1948], M. Louis Lumière, whose health had been steadily declining since 1946, was kind enough to allow me to interview him for the French television service....

A lengthy afternoon's work was required. M. Louis Lumière, who at that time scarcely left his bed, had to make a considerable physical effort in reading, at the cost of great exertion, the text which he held before his almost sightless eyes. However, under the projectors and in front of the microphone he maintained his usual smiling affability. This was the last time he was confronted by the apparatus on which he had bestowed the name "Cinéma."

Last March [1948] this interview was televised: it opened the series of remarkable broadcasts which Georges Charensol devoted to the history of the cinema, with the collaboration of Pierre Brive. It is thanks to their initiative that the cinema is able to retain among its archives a final picture—and an extremely touching one—of Louis Lumière.

SADOUL: M. Louis Lumière, what were the circumstances in which you began to be interested in animated photography?

LOUIS LUMIERE: It was during the summer of 1894 that my brother Auguste and I commenced our first work. At that period, the research of Marey, Edison, and Démeny had caused those inventors to arrive at certain results, but no projection of film on a screen had yet been accomplished.

The main problem to be solved was that of finding a system of driving the strip of film pictures. My brother Auguste had thought of using for the purpose an indented cylinder, similar to that proposed by Léon Boully in another apparatus. But such a system was clumsy. It couldn't work and never did.

SADOUL: Did M. Auguste Lumière then put forward other systems?

LOUIS LUMIERE: No, my brother ceased being interested in the technical side of the cinematograph as soon as I had found the right driving device. If the cinematograph patent was taken out in our joint name, this was because we always signed jointly the work reported on and the patents we filed, whether or not both of us took part in the work. *I was actually the sole author of the cinematograph,* just as he on his side was the creator of other inventions that were always patented in both our names....

SADOUL: Did you have to wait long before using celluloid films similar to those employed by the modern cinema?

LOUIS LUMIERE: I would have used celluloid strips at once had I been able to obtain in France a flexible, transparent celluloid which gave me satisfaction. However, no French or British firm was then making any. I had to send one of our departmental managers to the United States, who purchased celluloid in nonsensitized sheets from the New York Celluloid Company, and brought them back to us at Lyon. We cut them and perforated them with the aid of an apparatus whose feed device was based on that of a sewing machine, which apparatus was perfected by M. Moisson.

SADOUL: What was the date when you were able to make your first film on celluloid?

LOUIS LUMIERE: It was at the end of the summer of 1894 that I was able to make my first film, *Workers Leaving the*

Lumière Factory. As you may have noticed, the men are wearing straw hats and the women summer dresses. Moreover, I needed strong sunlight to be able to make such scenes, for my lens was not very powerful, and I should not have been able to take such a view in winter or at the end of autumn. The film was shown in public for the first time at Paris, rue de Rennes, before the Société d'Encouragement pour l'Industrie Nationale. This was on March 22, 1895. This showing ended a lecture which I had been asked to give by the illustrious physicist, Mascart, of the Institute, then President of the Society. I also showed on the screen the formation of a photographic image in course of development: this involved certain difficulties that I won't go into here.

SADOUL: Was your apparatus already called the cinematograph?

LOUIS LUMIERE: I do not think we had already baptized it. Our first patent, taken out on February 13, 1895, did not adopt any particular name. In that patent we merely referred to "an apparatus for obtaining and showing chronophotographic prints." It was not until several weeks afterwards that we selected the name cinematograph....

SADOUL: Did the perfection of your cinematograph involve you in technical problems that were difficult to solve?

LOUIS LUMIERE: One of the points which received my attention was that of the resistance of the films. Celluloid films were then, to us, a new product of whose qualities or properties we were ignorant. I therefore embarked on methodical experiments by piercing the strips with needles of different diameters, to which I suspended increasing weights. I thus arrived at important conclusions, for instance that the hole might, without inconvenience, be larger than the pin passing through it and have equally as good resistance as if the hole and the pin were the same size....

SADOUL: Since in 1895 you only had a single apparatus which served both for taking pictures and for showing them, during that year you were the sole operator taking pictures for your cinematograph?

LOUIS LUMIERE: That is correct. All the films which were shown in 1895, either at the Photographic Congress of Lyon in June, for the Revue Générale des Sciences in Paris in July, or in Paris, the basement of the Grand-Café, from December 28, 1895, onwards, were films for which I had been the operator. There was a single exception: *Les Bruleuses d'Herbes* [*The Grass Burners*] was taken by my brother Auguste, who was on holiday at our estate in La Ciotat. I should add that not only did I make these films, but the first strips shown at the Grand-Café were developed by me in enameled iron slop-buckets containing the developer, then the washing water and the fixative. The relevant positives were similarly printed and I used as source of light a white wall with the sun shining on it.

SADOUL: Can you, M. Lumière, tell us about the *Partie d'Ecarté* [*The Card Game*]?

LOUIS LUMIERE: The partners are: my father, Antoine Lumière, who lights a cigar. Opposite him, his friend the conjurer Trewey, who is dealing the cards. Trewey was, moreover, the organizer in London of showings of our cinematograph, and he is to be seen in several of the films, *Assiettes Tournantes* [*Spinning Plates*] for instance. The third player, who is pouring out some beer, is my father-in-law, the brewer Winkler of Lyon. The servant, finally, was a man attached to the house. He was born at Confaron—a pure-blooded southern Frenchman, full of gaiety and wit, who kept us amused with his repartee and jokes.

L'Arrivée du Train en Gare [*The Arrival of a Train at a Station*], which I took at the station of La Ciotat in 1895, shows on the platform a little girl who is skipping along, one hand held by her mother and the other by her nurse. The child is my eldest daughter, afterwards Mrs. Trarieux, and she is now four times a grandmother. My mother, Mrs. Antoine Lumière, can be identified by her Scotch cape.

SADOUL: What can you tell us about the famous *Arroseur Arrosé* [*The Sprinkler Sprinkled*]?

LOUIS LUMIERE: Although my recollections are not very accurate, I think I may say that the idea of the scenario was suggested to me by a farce by my younger brother Edouard, whom we unhappily lost while an airman during the 1914–1918 war. He was then too young to play the part of the urchin who treads on the garden hose. I replaced him by a young apprentice from the carpentry workshop of the factory, Duval, who died after performing his duties as chief packer of the works for almost forty-two years. As regards the waterer, the part was played by our gardener M. Clerc, who is still alive after being employed by the works for forty years. He is retired and is now living near Valence.

SADOUL: How many films did you make in 1895?

LOUIS LUMIERE: I must have made nearly fifty. My memory is not very reliable with regard to the number of these subjects. These films were all 17 meters long and it took about a minute to show them. This length of 17 meters may seem odd, but it was merely governed by the capacity of the spool-boxes holding the negative film when the pictures were taken.

SADOUL: Can you mention a few titles of films which you made in 1895?

LOUIS LUMIERE: We produced a few comic films in which relations, friends, employees, etc., took part.... I should also mention the "Landing of Members of the Congress" at Neuville-sur-Saône, which was in a way the first news film, for I took it on the occasion of the Photographic Congress in June, 1895, and showed it next day before the members of the congress.

SADOUL: Have you made any films since 1895?

LOUIS LUMIERE: Very few. I left this to the operators whom I had trained: Promio, Mesguich, Doublier, Perrigot, and others. In a few years they had entered in our catalogs over twelve hundred films made in all parts of the world.

SADOUL: How long is it since you have ceased to be interested in the cinematograph?

LOUIS LUMIERE: My last work dates back to 1935, at which time I perfected a stereoscopic cinema which was shown, in particular, at Paris, Lyon, Marseille, and Nice. However, my work has been in the direction of scientific research. I have never engaged in what is termed "production." I do not think I would fit into a modern studio. Moreover, I have been incapacitated for some time and can scarcely leave Bandol.

Sight and Sound
Summer 1948

The World of Ideas

The interplay of ideas bears analysis, whether it is the impact of a farsighted work of fiction on an inventor or the influence of the true-life story of an ill-fated device on a filmmaker.

In The Time Machine *(1895), British writer H. G. Wells recounts the adventures of a man who invents a machine that travels in time. Some of his descriptions are fairly cinematic: "I think I have told you that when I set out, before my velocity became very high, Mrs. Watchett had walked across the room, travelling, as it seemed to me, like a rocket. As I returned, I passed again across that minute when she traversed the laboratory. But now her every motion appeared to be the exact inversion of her previous ones. The door at the lower end opened, and she glided quietly up the laboratory, back foremost, and disappeared behind the door by which she had previously entered."* The Time Machine *had a profound effect on many—and in particular on Robert W. Paul, who referred to it and consulted the author before preparing the following patent application.*

A Novel Form of Exhibition or Entertainment, Means for Presenting the Same

My invention consists of a novel form of exhibition whereby the spectators have presented to their view scenes which are supposed to occur in the future or the past, while they are given the sensation of voyaging upon a machine through time, and means for presenting these scenes simultaneously and in conjunction with the production of the sensations by the mechanism described below, or its equivalent.

The mechanism I employ consists of a platform, or platforms, each of which contain a suitable number of spectators and which may be enclosed at the sides after the spectators have taken their places, leaving a convenient opening towards which the latter face, and which is directed towards a screen upon which the views are presented.

In order to create the impression of traveling, each platform may be suspended from cranks in shafts above the platform, which may be driven by an engine or other convenient source of power. These cranks may be so placed as to impart to the platform a gentle rocking motion, and may also be employed to cause the platform to travel bodily forward through a short space, when desired, or I may substitute for this portion of the mechanism similar shafts below the platforms, provided with cranks or cams, or worms keyed eccentrically on the shaft, or wheels gearing in racks attached to the underside of the platform or otherwise.

Simultaneously with the forward propulsion of the platform, I may arrange a current of air to be blown over it, either by fans attached to the sides of the platform, and intended to represent to the spectators the means of propulsion, or by a separate blower driven from the engine and arranged to throw a blast over each of the platforms.

After the starting of the mechanism, and a suitable period having elapsed, representing, say, a certain number of centuries, during which the platforms may be in darkness, or in alternations of darkness and dim light, the mechanism may be slowed and a pause made at a given epoch, on which the scene upon the screen will come gradually into view of the spectators, increasing in size and distinctness from a small vista, until the figures, etc., may appear lifelike if desired.

In order to produce a realistic effect, I prefer to use for the projection of the scene upon the screen, a number of powerful lanterns, throwing the respective portions of the picture, which may be composed of,

(1) A hypothetical landscape, containing also the representations of the inanimate objects in the scene.

(2) A slide, or slides, which may be traversed horizontally or vertically and contain representations of objects such as a navigable balloon, etc., which is required to traverse the scene.

(3) Slides or films, representing in successive instantaneous photographs, after the manner of the kinetoscope, the living persons or creatures in their natural motions....

(4) Changeable coloured, darkened, or perforated slides may be used to produce the effect on the scene of sunlight, darkness, moonlight, rain, etc.

In order to enable the scenes to be gradually enlarged to a definite amount, I may mount these lanterns on suitable carriages or trolleys, upon rails provided with stops or marks, so as to approach to or recede from the screen a definite distance, and to enable a dissolving effect to be obtained, the lantern may be fitted with the usual mechanism. In order to increase the realistic effect I may arrange that after a certain number of scenes from a hypothetical future have been presented to the spectators, they may be allowed to step from the platforms, and be conducted through grounds or buildings arranged to represent exactly one of the epochs through which the spectator is supposed to be traveling.

After the last scene is presented I prefer to arrange that the spectators should be given the sensation of voyaging backwards from the last epoch to the present, or the present epoch may be supposed to have been

The departure of Raoul Grimoin-Sanson's balloon drew crowds in the Tuileries Gardens in Paris.

accidentally passed, and a past scene represented on the machine coming to standstill, after which the impression of traveling forward again to the present epoch may be given, and the re-arrival notified by the representation on the screen of the place at which the exhibition is held, or of some well-known building which by the movement forward of the lantern can be made to increase gradually in size as if approaching the spectator.

Robert W. Paul
British patent application no. 19984
24 October 1895

There is a curious analogy to be drawn between Raoul Grimoin-Sanson's balloon cinema and the adventures of Professor Mabouloff, the hero of one of Georges Méliès's lost films, outlined here.

The Fantastic Dirigible, or The Inventor's Nightmare

Overcome by a great lassitude due to long, hard work and experiments on the problem of aerial navigation, an inventor decides to take a rest, especially since he thinks he has arrived at the perfect solution—a marvelous flying machine. He stretches out and falls asleep almost immediately. While he is sound asleep, he finds that a magic spell has been cast that covers his balloon in a net, and he helplessly watches the destruction of the plans on which he has spent his days and nights, the annihilation of his life's ambition. Little by little, he calms down. He then sees his balloon take flight, the motor running. It rises, moving easily, a total master of the air, while the clouds pass by at great speed. His overexcited mind imagines strange, indistinct forms inhabiting his balloon. These forms take the shape of women who abandon the machine to wheel about in the air. A comet with an incandescent tail crosses the sky. With horror, he sees it approach the balloon, which is filled with inflam-

Vers les Etoiles (Toward the Stars), a 1908 film by Georges Méliès.

mable gas. The inevitable collision results, followed by an enormous explosion.

Nothing now remains of the marvelous invention which was supposed to make the name Mabouloff known to posterity. All these imaginary noises end up awakening our inventor, who finds himself in the middle of his laboratory. But the vision seemed so real to him that he is convinced that his device no longer exists. Demoralized and beaten, he throws himself out of the window. This scene is absolutely spectacular due to the ingeniousness of the singularly strange inventions around a subject that fascinates by its possibilities and its dangers. A great film for its color effects.

158 Scénarios of Lost Films
by Georges Méliès,
1986

Tricks of the Trade

Those who worked in the cinema did not like to reveal the secrets of a profession whose practices were learned by long apprenticeship. Nevertheless, in 1906, Georges Méliès agreed to write a long article in which he mixed general principles and hands-on experience. Cecil Hepworth described his ideal studio in his memoirs.

You have to put, as we say, a hand to the plow, and for a long while, in order to really understand the innumerable difficulties to be overcome in a craft that consists of doing everything, even if it seems impossible, and of giving the appearance of reality to the most chimerical dreams, the most improbable inventions of the imagination. Finally, needless to say, it is absolutely necessary to *realize the impossible*, since you are photographing it, and you must make it seen! For the special genre that concerns us here, it was necessary to create a studio prepared *ad hoc*. In a word, it was the meeting of a photographic studio (in giant proportions) and a theater. The construction is of iron, glassed-in; at one end you find the cabin for the

George Albert Smith's studio in Brighton, England, opened up completely so as to benefit from the daylight.

camera and operator, while at the other end a stage built exactly like those in theaters, divided like them into flaps, trapdoors, and cuts in the flooring. Of course, on each side of the set there are wings, with storage rooms for sets, and behind, dressing rooms for the performers and extras. The scene includes an underground area with the trapdoors and the buffers necessary to make infernal divinities in the fairy films appear and disappear; false alleys through which the trusses are collapsed when the scene changes, and a grid overhead with drums and winches necessary for maneuvers requiring strength (flying characters or chariots, oblique flights for angels, fairies, or swimmers, etc.). Special drums serve for maneuvering the panoramic backdrops; electric projectors light and activate apparitions. In summary, it is, in miniature, a rather faithful reproduction of a theater for fairy stories. The stage is about ten meters wide, plus three meters of wings in the courtyard and garden. The total length, from the stage apron to the camera, is seventeen meters. Outside, there are ironwork workshops for construction of accessories, practicable scenery, etc., and a series of storerooms for construction materials, accessories, and costumes.

Lighting by Day and Artificial Light

The ceiling of the studio is partly covered with frosted glass and partly with ordinary glass. In summer, if the sun struck the sets through the glass panes, the effect would be disastrous, with the shadows of the ironwork roof showing up violently on the backdrops. Therefore, a set of mobile shutters operated by wires that can open and close them in the wink of an eye are used to ward off this danger. The shutters' frame is covered with tracing material used by architects to design their plans; when they are closed, this gives a softened light, similar to that of frosted glass. Regular light is extremely difficult to obtain during the execution of a scene, which can last four consecutive hours and more, for a subject which in projection will last two to four minutes. So, during cloudy weather, when the cursed black cumulus clouds take pleasure in passing constantly in front of the sun, that friend of the photographer, exasperation is not long in manifesting itself in the person who is directing the operators, aides, machinists, actors, and extras. Endless patience is necessary: sometimes to wait until daylight wishes to return, sometimes to close the shutters if there is too much light or open them again if there is not enough, and all this without losing sight of the thousand details of the work at hand. If I am not crazy today, I will never become so, since the fleecy, cloudy, or foggy skies sorely tried my patience… and caused me, during my career, countless failures, accompanied by enormous expense, since any scene begun again or impossible to play as a result of bad weather means that actors have been inconvenienced, at double, triple, or quadruple the cost price, according to whether we start over two, three, or four days in a row. I have seen scenes played eight consecutive days— among others, the ballet from *Faust*, which lasts two and a half minutes and cost 3,200 francs. That was something to get furious about.

In addition, after much trial and error—and although it had often been declared impossible—I succeeded quite recently, using a special electric installation composed of stage lights, trained and upright (as in the theaters) in creating artificial lighting that gives the absolute effect of daylight, and which will finally spare me, in the future, from the rude experiences of the past. God be praised! I will not go crazy…at least due to the clouds.… The diffuse light is obtained with the aid of a very large number of arc lamps and tubes of mercury vapor suitably combined. This artificial light is employed concurrently with the daylight, and the intensity can be varied at will according to need.

Composition and Preparation of Scenes

The composition of a scene, whether of a play, drama, fairy story, comedy, or an artistic scene, naturally demands the creation of a scenario drawn from the imagination; then the search for the effects that will move the audience; the development of sketches and models of the sets and costumes; and the creation of the highlighted shot, without which no other shot has a chance of succeeding. When one is dealing with illusions or fairy stories, this shot, the combination of devices, the sketches for trick effects, and the study preliminary to their construction all demand special care. The direction is similarly prepared in advance, as are the movements of the extras and the placing of the actors. It is a task absolutely analogous to the preparation of a stage play; with the difference that the author must himself know how to combine everything on paper, and be, in consequence, the author, director, designer, and often actor, if he wishes to obtain a whole

that hangs together. The inventor of the scene must direct it himself, because it is absolutely impossible to make it succeed if ten different people meddle. Above all it is necessary to know exactly what you want and throw yourself into all the others' roles. You must not lose sight of the fact that you cannot rehearse for three months as in a theater, but for a quarter of an hour at the most. If you waste time, the day wanes…and good-by to the shooting. Everything must be anticipated, even and especially the pitfalls to avoid in the course of execution—and, in scenes done with machinery, there are many of those.

Actors and Extras

Contrary to what is generally believed, it is very difficult to find good actors for the motion pictures. One actor, excellent in the theater, even a star, is worth absolutely nothing in a film scene. Often even professional mimes are bad, because they play pantomime with the conventional principles, just as the ballet mimes do a special kind of performing which is immediately recognized. These artistes, superior in their own specialty, are uncomfortable when they come near motion pictures. This derives from the fact that cinematographic gestures demand special qualities and study in themselves. Here there is no audience to whom the actor speaks, whether verbally or in mime. Only the camera is the spectator, and nothing is worse than watching it and worrying about it while one is performing, which is exactly what invariably happens the first time to actors accustomed to the theater and not to the motion pictures. The actor must imagine that he should make himself understood, while remaining mute, by the "deaf" people who are watching him. His playing must be sober, very expressive; few gestures, but very clear and precise ones. Perfect play of facial expression and very appropriate postures are indispensable. I have seen numerous scenes played by well-known actors; they were not good, because the principal element of their success, the spoken word, was lacking in the motion pictures. Accustomed to speaking well, they employed the gesture only as an accessory to theatrical speech, whereas in the motion pictures the word is nothing, the gesture everything. Some of them, nevertheless, have done good scenes, Galipaux among others. Why? Because he is used to the solo mime in his monologues, and he is gifted with the most expressive face. He knows how to make himself understood without speaking, and his gestures, even voluntarily exaggerated (which is necessary in pantomime and especially in photo-graphed pantomime) are always most accurate. No matter how accurate an actor's gesture when it accompanies his speech, it is not at all comprehensible when he mimes. If you say "I am thirsty" in the theater, you will not bring your thumb with a closed hand to your mouth to simulate a bottle. It is quite useless, since the whole world has understood that you are thirsty. But, in pantomime, you would obviously be obliged to make this gesture.

It is really quite simple, isn't it? Well, nine times out of ten, this will not occur to anyone who is not used to miming. Nothing can be improvised, everything must be learned. There is need, too, for taking account of what the camera is showing. When

characters find themselves, in a shot, pressed on top of each other, you always have to pay the greatest attention to separating the principal characters off toward the front and moderating the ardor of secondary characters, who are always inclined to gesticulate inappropriately—this has the effect of producing on the screen a muddle of people fidgeting, and the audience no longer knows whom to watch and doesn't understand the action. The phases should be successive, not simultaneous. From this comes the necessity for the actors to be attentive and play their roles in turn and only at the precise moment when their participation becomes necessary. This is another thing that I have often had a hard time making actors understand, since they are always inclined to show themselves off and be noticed, to the great detriment of the action and the whole cast; generally, they have too much goodwill. And what kid gloves you must wear to moderate this eagerness without offending them! As strange as it seems, each actor of the rather numerous troupe that I employ has been chosen from among twenty or thirty whom I tested without obtaining what was wanted, though they were all very fine artistes in the Paris theaters from which they came....

Difficulties and Drawbacks

Besides the obstacles mentioned above, that is, the difficulties inherent in the execution of these sorts of scenes, there are others that occur to hamper the cinematographer: these include the variation in light, clouds passing over the sun, accidents with the equipment, the filmstock getting stuck, the tearing of overly thin film, the emulsion's lack of sensitivity, the spots or sparkle are found on some films after developing, which renders them unusable, in which holes imperceptible to the naked eye are transformed into sizable stones in the enlarged projection. What a relief it is after developing to realize that the shot was perfect! No laymen will understand the doses of patience, perseverance, and strong will necessary for success; and I cannot stop myself from smiling when I hear "How come these views cost so much?" I know only too well why; but how can we make this understood by someone who does not know how this work is done and who takes away from a shot only one thing: the cheapness!

Shooting: The Cameraman

It goes without saying that the camera operator for this special genre must be very skillful and very informed about a host of the small tricks of the trade. A difficult view cannot be shot by a beginner. He would invariably ruin the most able accomplished effects if he forgot the smallest detail in turning the crank. One mistake in turning, forgetting one number in counting out loud while he is taking the shot, a momentary distraction—can spoil everything. It takes a calm, attentive, thoughtful man, capable of resisting all irritations and annoyances. Irritations and annoyances are almost inevitable when one is shooting, with innumerable difficulties and disagreeable surprises occurring almost continually. These few observations will make it comprehensible why the shooting of fantasy scenes, depending at once on the director, the stagehands, the actors, and the operator taking the scene, is so difficult. It requires perfect agreement, everyone's attention, and exact cooperation—which are scarcely easy to obtain, while one is fighting against material problems of all sorts.

This will suffice to explain why, after having thrown themselves into this new genre, most cameramen have given it up. You have to be something other than a simple operator to do all this; and, while there are plenty of cameramen, those who have succeeded in making something finer than the others are few and far between: at most one per country, and yet almost all countries of the world are dependent on French manufacturers for artistic scenes.

Georges Méliès
"Cinematographic Views," 1907

It was shortly after *Rescued by Rover*—and perhaps because or on account of it, for it brought considerable grist to the mill—that I began to contemplate building an indoor studio for film-making. This was in the summer of 1905. I had nothing to go upon because so far as I knew then, or indeed, so far as I know now, there was no studio in existence and working at that time. So all the conditions had to be envisaged and the detail thrashed out in my own mind. There was no thought at all of a "dark" studio; what I wanted was one that would let in as much as possible of the daylight while protecting us from rain and wind, but it must not cast any shadows. Ordinary window-glass would let through the maximum of light, but in sunshine there must always be the shadows of the wood or iron bars in which the glass is mounted. So I set about looking for a glass which would diffuse the sunshine and so kill the shadows but without greatly diminishing the amount of the light. After considerable experiment I hit upon Muranese glass which exactly fulfilled these conditions. It gives beautifully smooth flood-lighting but cuts off no more light-value than ordinary glass.

But I realised, of course, that sunshine cannot be relied upon and I wanted to avoid the inconvenience of having to wait upon its vagaries. So I rigged up in our back garden—where all of this sort of thing had perforce to be done—an electric arc-lamp and tested as well as I could what additional help we might expect from this source. The result was our first studio. It was so shaped that the daylight could reach the acting floor from every reasonable point, including the space over the cameras, and, in addition, there was a row of hanging automatic arc-lamps and some on stands which could be wheeled about into various positions.

It was some very considerable time after this that all the principal American producers abandoned New York and shifted three thousand miles across their continent to Los Angeles so as to have almost continuous sunlight, and then, as soon as they got there, dug themselves into dark studios to keep the sunlight out! I couldn't make sense of this at first but I came to realise that what they really wanted to avoid was the hourly *shifting* of the sunlight, constantly altering the values of their pre-arranged scenery. Still, they could have accomplished all that by remaining on the East side, where all actors, technicians and supplies were ready to their hands. Expense is wrought by want of thought as well as want of art.

Our studio was built at first-floor height so as to be that much above the level of surrounding houses, and the space underneath was devoted to three printing and developing machines— same old pattern—drying-rooms, mechanics' shops and so on. One small room in front between the main dark-room and the road was the perforating room with half a dozen motor-driven Debrie perforators, for it was not until considerably later that the filmstock makers took over the perforating as part of their responsibility.

It is curious to note how little faith is put by builders and folk of that sort in the ideas of people who are young and inexperienced but not necessarily silly. I designed this small building, made the plans and all necessary drawings and submitted them for an estimate to a local builder of good repute. His first response was to say, "That roof won't work; it can't be built; it will 'wind'." I didn't agree but in the end I had to make a scale model in cardboard to prove that I was right.

Then again, I had allowed a space of six feet square for a staircase turning three right-angles to the first floor. He made no comment on this but just altered the measurement to six-by-*eight* feet. But a staircase of this description, whatever its size, must be square at its base. When the building was up he found this out and had to put in an additional inner wall in accord with my measurement, and that two feet of wasted space is there to this day.

When the studio was built and ready for work I put down a sort of railway for the wheeled camera-stand to run on, to make what are now called "tracking shots," which had not by then been heard of. Also we used a panoramic head so as to follow the actors as they moved about the scene, until we were informed by America—then our biggest customer—that Americans would not stand these movements and we must keep the camera stationary. Think of American films today when the camera is scarcely ever still for two seconds at a time!

I don't say the Americans learned anything from us for that is not at all likely, but I do say that we learned a very great deal from them, though I for one admit that I learned too slowly. Brought up in the stage tradition it seemed to me for years that in all general views you must photograph your actors as they appear on the stage, full length from head right down to feet, and only in admitted close-ups could you omit unnecessary limbs. But the American films unblushingly cut them off at the knees or even higher when they could show important details more easily that way. It looked all wrong to me at first but I soon gave way and adopted the new technique. The American films which were beginning to come over in quantities about then, showed also far better photographic quality, particularly in definition, indicating much better lenses than we were using. So we had to hunt around for better lenses, which soon brought us to the German opticians and their wonderful Jena glass.

Cecil M. Hepworth,
Came the Dawn: Memories of a Film Pioneer, 1951

I n *How It Feels To Be Run Over* (1900) Hepworth shows the film cameraman being run over by a car. Notes scratched directly on the film translate his last impressions.

The First Woman Filmmaker

Alice Guy started as the secretary to Léon Gaumont, who was then manufacturing cameras. The mark she made on the young motion-picture industry was much grander than either of them ever would have predicted.

As the daughter of a publisher, I had read a lot and remembered little. I had done some amateur theater and thought it could be done better. Building up my courage, I asked Gaumont if I could write one or two playlets, and to have them acted by friends of mine. Had we known what the idea would develop into, I would never have received his authorization.

Considering my age, my lack of experience, my gender, I had nothing going for me. But he did give me his permission, as long as none of this impinged upon my secretarial duties. I had to get to the office at 8 AM, open, register, and distribute the mail. I was then allowed to take the omnibus, drawn by four horses, which climbed the Buttes Chaumont via the Rue La Fayette. I could then make the most of the time allotted to me. At 4:30 PM I had to be back at St. Roch to take dictation, get things signed, etc. This often took until 10 or 11 at night. Then, I could at last go home to the Quai Malaquais for a few hours' sleep, which I considered well earned.

Léon Gaumont found that I was wasting too much time with my comings and goings. He offered to fix up a small house he owned at the end of the Rue des Sonneries, behind the photography laboratory....

Sensing my hesitation, he promised to install a bathroom and to get a gardener from the Buttes Chaumont to clean up the garden. I ended up giving in. I'd been bitten by the cinema bug. Full of regret, we left our attic room on the Quai Malaquais....

I was given an unused terrace with an asphalt floor (making it impossible to fix a real set). It was covered with a shaky glass roof and overlooked an empty lot. In this palace, I made my debut as a director. A sheet painted by a neighborhood painter who specialized primarily in scarecrows and the like; a vague set—rows of cabbage constructed by a carpenter; costumes rented around the Porte St. Martin. The cast: my friends, a crying baby, a worried mother. My first film, *La Fée aux Choux* [*The Cabbage Fairy*], thus saw the light. Today it is considered a classic. The Cinémathèque Française has the negative.

I'd be going overboard if I told you it was a masterpiece, but the public wasn't blasé and the actors were young and charming. The film was enough of a success that I was allowed to try again.

Thanks to the goodwill of my small staff; thanks to the advice and lessons of Frédéric Dillaye (technical advisor to the Gaumont Corporation and the author of excellent books on art photography); thanks to the experience garnered day by day; and thanks to luck and chance—we discovered hundreds of little tricks of the trade. Here are a few of them:

Shooting the film backwards allowed houses being demolished to reconstruct themselves by pure magic; or a person falling from a roof to soar back up spontaneously; or a hungry client in a cake shop, having found the check too pricey, to return the already-eaten pastries intact.

Slowing down or speeding up the crank could turn relaxed pedestrians into frenetic madmen or sleepwalkers.

Stopping the film allowed us to move an object which, during projection, seemed endowed with supernatural powers: an archaeologist could thus be stupefied to find his precious mummy playing in the four corners of his laboratory. Example: *The Mummy.*

Shooting from different distances made it possible to place in the same frame both pygmies and giants, as in *Lilliput and Gulliver, The Ogre and Tom Thumb*, and *The Grandfather Clock's Cakewalk.*

Double exposures.

Dissolves used for visions and dreams.

We also made some movies on location. During a walk in Barbizon, we came across an old stagecoach. I decided to direct *The Mail from Lyon.* A theatrical troupe would have been too expensive, so I persuaded my staff to play the parts. Armed with a copious homemade lunch, costumes, props, and a bicycle for almost everyone, we took the train to Melun. At the station, two or three cars, with drivers claiming to be guides to the Fontainebleau forest, took the less athletic young women and the packages. We all set off for Barbizon, where the stagecoach was awaiting us.

The guides took us to a place they considered appropriate. After having savored our picnic, we handed out the costumes. The women did their best behind bushes. The men, less prim, got dressed anywhere. Fortunately, the forest was empty, because we must have been quite a strange sight....

Despite the brisk autumn weather, our venture was a success. We were full of joy and good humor, and we decided to do it again.

All these short films (of 17 to 25 meters), shot in incredible circumstances, contained the seeds of today's cinema.

Alice Guy
*Autobiography of a Film Pioneer
(1873–1968)*, 1976

War Films

Camera operators assigned to film the great international conflicts led a life only slightly less dangerous than the combatants and sometimes even took part in the engagements.

In 1898 Billy Bitzer Was Sent to Cuba to Cover the Spanish-American War—His First—With a Particularly Awkward Biograph Camera

The Biograph movie camera was out after scoops called "News Happenings," when word came that the U.S. Navy battleship *Maine* had been blown up in Havana Harbor, so I was sent with my cumbersome camera to cover the story.

I embarked upon the *Seguranca*, reaching Havana on February 19, 1898, four days after the news broke. On Wednesday morning we sighted in the distance old Morro Castle, a sheer two hundred feet above the sea. To the left of Morro was La Sohaca, and ahead stretched a winding waterway bordered by palm-fringed shores. At the entrance to the bay we passed Estrella Point and Cayo Smith, a

A cameraman from the Charles Urban Trading Company with a Bioscope.

The sailors of the *Potemkin* led a workers' uprising in Odessa in 1905. The story quickly became the subject of a Pathé reconstruction.

picturesque, hilly islet. It was then we came abreast of the battleship *Maine*, an unrecognizable mass of scrap iron, twisted and mangled. Only a single hulk remained, from which flew the American flag, in what appeared defiance of those who had destroyed her.

Visiting Cuba under Spanish rule was highly dangerous. With bag and baggage we were hustled into the Customs House. My camera was bulky enough, but when you consider it was driven by a motor operated by over two thousand pounds of storage batteries, packed in many boxes, which the officials insisted on examining, all this took much time. The grins and leers on the faces of bystanders gave me to

understand this was unfriendly territory. Luckily I had been warned beforehand to go straight to the Ingleterra Hotel, where I would find comfort and safety. As I learned later, it was well for me that I was one to follow orders. After checking in at the hotel, I went back to the wreckage of the *Maine* to take pictures.

Divers were at work recovering bodies—at one end Spanish divers, and at the other Americans. I knew it would be impossible for me, with my bulky camera, to get pictures that would tell the true story, but our boys with still cameras did such admirable work that today in the photo section of the Library of Congress you are able to see it for yourself. All I got was moving

During the Boer War, the soldiers' life was captured by the lens of Joseph Rosenthal.

pictures of the *Maine* as seen from the shore.

I remained in Havana, trying to get pictures from a towboat, and then we were ordered back to New York on the same day Ambassador Fitzhugh Lee evacuated Havana. In New York they kept me busy on "News Happenings," and it was not until April 21 (my twenty-sixth birthday, incidentally) that I returned, as war was then declared by the United States.

I happened to be in Boston covering more news when the Biograph office telegraphed that arrangements had been made with the New York *Journal* for several newsmen, two still photographers, and myself with the movie outfit to go aboard a towboat to cover the war in Cuba. This time my journey took me to Siboney, the point where our battleships had cleared out the Spanish to make a landing for our troops. I took some shots of the troops landing from the "Yale" and "Harvard" transports, and other shots along the beach.

I found myself helpless to advance with the troops because of the scarcity of horses. Horses had been shipped all right, but most of them had drowned. The horses had simply been pushed overboard without anyone holding up their heads, and the weight of a horse in rough water was too much. They had drowned because no one there knew how to handle the situation before it got out of hand.

Those in charge of the landing had been greatly at fault.

Without means of transportation to follow the troops, I returned to my towboat, where we stationed ourselves, taking pictures each morning as the battleships in Havana harbor fired on the sand batteries about Morro Castle. Through binoculars we could see the clouds of sand and what seemed to be bodies of men and fragments of guns flying in the air toward us. At this point we were ordered out to sea, with threats of arrest if we came in line of the battleship fire again. We stationed ourselves three miles out, in international waters, awaiting a reprieve. I was relieved by this, remembering a near-miss shell that struck the water just a little in front of us and ricocheted over my head. I had pulled the focusing cloth I was using just a little further over my head, like a damn fool, but continued grinding out the action nevertheless.

We remained on the towboat waiting for the big naval battle that was rumored. We were growing impatient when one morning a crew man shook us awake: "Your big boss is outside, it's time to get up." Then I saw the yacht *Sylvia* standing across the water, so we were taken over to her. Aboard was William Randolph Hearst of the New York *Journal,* accompanied by Jack Follansbee, James Creelman, and two pretty young ladies who were sisters. It looked mighty inviting after all the tedious hours we had spent.

Here were champagne and lively companionship. One still-cameraman of our party needed ice in developing his plates, and here we had plenty of ice. This change from the smell of tar rope and oil and the confined quarters of the towboat was the best remedy we could have to relieve tension and refresh our spirits.

The *Sylvia* had just arrived that morning, and they were all anxious to go sightseeing. This would be difficult if the girls were seen by the sailors on the battleships, so to prevent this, the girls donned male attire. We were in the delirious state of being under fire in war time, and we got more friendly than we would have at home; the crew mixed with the guests and vice versa.

Having discovered that the Spanish fleet was lying at anchor in Havana harbor, our fleet, the North American Squadron, promptly bottled their exit by sinking the *Merrimac* across the entrance of the harbor. I could not get pictures, as this took place at night.

I decided at this juncture to land with my Frankenstein-like camera and exert new efforts to obtain battle scenes. Frederic Remington, who was returning to the States, gave me his horse to view the prospects and pull the camera ashore. Then I was ready to follow the troops inland. The outposts were within a few miles of Havana, so I started with my camera toward General William R. Shafter's headquarters, halfway between my starting point and the front line.

I took movies of the general with his staff, crossing a stream on horseback. He was a portly gentleman and filled the area of the postal-card movie field so well that it was unnecessary to worry about filling in the background.

G. W. Bitzer
Billy Bitzer: His Story
1973

The Birth of the Advertising Film

The first advertising films appeared, projected on screens in the open air, in New York in 1897 and Paris in 1898. Edwin Porter, Félix Mesguich, and Georges Méliès claim the paternity of this ingenious idea.

In the spring of 1897 Edwin S. Porter… found something that was truly new. Kuhn & Webster, from whom he had bought his Projectorscope and West Indian rights, were engaged in making the first advertising films. Porter was employed to handle the projection of these pictures on a screen billboard facing Broadway at Thirty-fourth street, Herald Square. The pictures were made for a Scotchman who conceived the idea and owned the venture. Although his name has been lost to memory, the merit of his advertising lingers in the recollection that his first account was the bonny, brave Haig & Haig highland whiskey.…

From nightfall until midnight Porter ground off the advertising films from a little coop on the top of the Pepper Building. The advertising was interlarded with short bits of current subjects and the brief topical snatches of the day. The machine was behind the screen, a large translucent fabric sheet.…

The exhibitors of motion pictures in the adjacent amusement houses were also displeased with this public broadcasting of their medium of profit. Somebody said a word at the Tenderloin police station.

A few nights went by and then Porter, looking out from his projection coop, in the midst of a showing, saw Inspector Chapman, the hero of the Seeley dinner raid, in all the glory of his side whiskers, coming stealthily over the roof, accompanied by a uniformed squad.

Porter was arrested on a charge of blocking traffic and marched to court. That was the end of the venture, the first showing of advertising films.

Terry Ramsaye,
A Million and One Nights: A History of the Motion Picture through 1925, 1926

Méliès played on the disproportion between objects and people for the purposes of advertising.

A vast advertising billboard was spread out on the third floor of a building on Boulevard Montmartre. A swiveling frame reproduced photographs as in a magic lantern. Pedestrians were scarcely interested in it and passed it by. It was, in my opinion, fruitless. I suddenly imagined that if it became animated, it would kindle the curiosity of Parisians much more.

The next day, I explained this concept to Mr. Vergnes, director of the agency, and having convinced him, I quickly left for Lyon to buy a variety of Lumière equipment, camera and projector. It was on 18 October 1898 that a luminous advertisement by means of cinema appeared for the first time, at 5 Boulevard Montmartre. Thereafter, many animated posters followed each other on that screen, starting with the one for "Ripolin."

I had got it right; from the first day, all the passersby raised their heads, the double-decker bus "Madeleine-Bastille" was immobilized, and vehicles came to a stop. A new creation was sufficient to conquer central Paris. Regulations should be made to prevent bottlenecks on the grand boulevards.

Then came the turn of the Compagnie des Wagons-Lits, which was promoting travel for tourists through its photos, very well chosen moreover, of the Pyrenees, Savoy, and the Côte d'Azur. A report of my proposals was sent by the company to the railway companies; it concerned simply taking panoramas of landscapes as they appeared from the doorway of a moving train.

The response of the P.L.M. Company reached me a week later, accompanied by a circular letter to agents of the network and a travel permit. I got the same facilities on the lines in the Midi. They authorized me to harness a special wagon to the front of the locomotive.

Thanks to a very simple arrangement adapted to my platform, the solidly fixed camera stuck out through an open window.

I began with the Côte d'Azur. Leaning over the viewfinder, I saw the coast go by at great speed. With their sudden changes, the rapid and rushing views look like colored images. I scarcely had time to admire the site when Saint-Raphael flew by under a dazzling sky. The locomotive galloped along, roared between the pines and crimson rocks of Trayas, and crossed the Estérel. After countless curves, it emerged at Cannes in the perfume of mimosas; the eye rested on the sea where the waves broke on the Croisette and the islets of Sainte-Marguerite and Saint-Honorat; then, in the rosy distance, the Cap d'Antibes grew blurry and disappeared.

When, in front of the locomotive, my carriage surged into the hurly-burly of the Nice station, I had the illusion of conducting the train. On the platforms, the passengers looked at me curiously, as if they suspected me of experimenting with a new mode of traction....

Thus at the beginning of the year 1899, the open-air screen of the Wagons-Lits Company in the Place de l'Opéra reflected the animated face of some corners of French soil.

Félix Mesguich
Cranking the Camera, 1933

The year 1898 did not close without Méliès having a new stroke of genius. Coming home one day, he said to Eugénie: "What a marvelous vehicle of propaganda the cinema is for all sorts of products! It would suffice to find an original idea to attract the public's attention, and, in the middle of the film, you could drop the name of the chosen product..." The advertising film had just been born!

A few days later, in fact, Méliès shot his first of such films. He installed on the balcony of the mezzanine of the Robert-Houdin Théâtre, just above the entrance door, a giant screen on which he projected, transparently, from his office, comic sketches that particularly attracted the public, since their screening was free. In general, the advertising message did not appear until the end of the scenario, once the audience was caught up in the action. Naturally, the films were paid for by the firms concerned.

Méliès immediately had more clients than he wanted. Thus, for example, he shot for the famous Bornibus mustard a scene in which he gave his imagination free rein, because even in advertising films, he remained the great Méliès. For Bornibus, he imagined a restaurant in which the clients argued and sprayed each other with mustard. Soon, the ground is strewn with mustard pots. You have to believe it is tasty when a dog starts to lick it greedily.

"To get a dog to lick a pot of mustard," Méliès recounted, "was not

M éliès's advertisement for Bornibus mustard, with the dog nowhere in sight.

easy. So I resorted to a trick: I replaced the mustard with chocolate cream, which merited the ardor of the good doggie.… After which appears Bornibus's slogan: 'Bornibus, its mustard and pickles, made as Mother Marianne would.'"

The impact on the gazers who sauntered along the Boulevard des Italiens was considerable. For each new client Méliès had an original idea. He sang the praises of many celebrated products of the era: Orbec beer, Picon apéritif, Delion hats, Menier chocolate, Widow Brunot's wax, John Dewar's whiskey, and many others. Naturally, in these films as in his other productions Georges Méliès used the already rather abundant form of the in-house star, Jehanne d'Alcy. Jehanne later remembered:

"I had done the Bornibus mustard, the Poulain chocolate. We were given a corset and twenty francs. A man had come along who had invented a so-called whalebone stiffener which was better than the usual corset whalebone and was less expensive. So there we were in pantaloons, with a corset. There was also a film on a product to make hair grow again. The actor, instead of putting the product on his head, poured it over his feet and he grew hair on his shoes."

Madeleine Malthète-Méliès
Méliès, the Enchanter, 1985

Eroticism in the Cinema

Even in the beginning, movies were not always family entertainment. The very first films made were often on such subjects as "the bride goes to bed," inspired by a postcard series. By the turn of the century, erotic movies constituted a formal and expected category in production company catalogues. This list is taken from the Pathé catalogue of the time.

Saucy Scenes of a Piquant Nature

(Do not admit children to the exhibition of these scenes)

770—*The Awakening of Chrysis*
(20 meters)
In an atmosphere of perfumes from the Orient, Chrysis awakens. A Negress lavishes her with care, while Chrysis languorously raises herself from her bed, her body still languid from sleep.

772—*The Judgment of Phryné*
(20 meters)
In the attack by an Arab sheik on a caravan, a beautiful young woman has been captured. She is brought before the sheik, who immediately summons his eunuchs, asking them if the new arrival is worthy of the harem. On their affirmative reply and after careful examination, the captive is admitted and led to the women's dwelling.

775—*Yvette and Pierreuse Going to Bed*
(20 meters)
The scene shows two very different
bedrooms. On the left, a prostitute,
whom a procurer mistreats, goes to bed,
half-dressed, in a sort of cubbyhole;
while on the right we see a richly
furnished room, occupied by a pretty
person who puts herself to bed.

776—*Yvette and Pierreuse Getting Up*
(20 meters)
Same decor as the preceding. The scene
shows a half-dressed suitor kissing
Yvette; she awakens and stretches at
great length; the servant brings
breakfast. Meanwhile, in her hovel
Pierreuse puts on her rags. The
procurer has already emptied her
pockets.

The music hall actress Louise Willy in *Le
Coucher de la Mariée* (*The Bride Goes to
Bed*), a postcard series reshot for the cinema.

777—*Adultery "In Flagrante Delicto"*
(15 meters)
The woman comes to a rendezvous, and
she is surprised there by her husband, the
police superintendent, and his agents.
The officer discovers the woman naked
in the bathroom, and the furious lover
throws himself on the husband, but is
held back by the police. (*Reproduction of
a famous painting by Garnier.*)

778—*Socialite in the Bath*
(20 meters)
A pretty woman in a bathroom removes
her clothing to enter a bathtub. The
servant comes in to help her.

780—*"L'Assommoir" by Emile Zola—
The Laundry Scene* (15 meters)
To our great satisfaction, we have been
able to render the famous scene offered
us by the celebrated realist novelist in
L'Assommoir in an even more lifelike
manner.

781—*Painter and Model (undressed)*
(20 meters)
A painter and a model who feels disgust
at getting undressed. The painter
manages to convince her and is given
over to suggestive touches.

782—*Facetious Painter* (20 meters)
In his studio, a painter who is a real
joker poses a pretty woman; she thumbs
her nose at him each time he turns his
back. The painter shows his subject the
canvas, on which he has drawn a cow.
The furious woman breaks the canvas
over his head.

783—*The Flea* (20 meters)
A pretty young person in a negligee is
looking for a flea. A play of expressions
and poses that is totally suggestive.

Film Libraries and Museums

In 1938 representatives of the Museum of Modern Art in New York, the National Archives in London, the film archives of the German Reich in Berlin, and the Cinémathèque Française in Paris met with an important goal. They wanted to join forces to help fight a battle each was already waging independently: to promote, exhibit, and conserve the cinema, in particular, silent films, which at the time were considered to be lacking in both commercial and artistic value—the recently developed talkies were overwhelmingly popular. The four were convinced that film has an artistic and aesthetic importance in addition to its historical and social value, and that it gives us important information about our past as well as our future. Together, they formed the International Federation of Film Archives (FIAF), which, based in Brussels, has many members around the world who share in common programs.

Film Libraries

The first films in the history of the cinema are conserved by specialized archives and cinematheques (film libraries), national institutions, private associations, and private collectors. A great number of films have nevertheless disappeared, and the safeguarding of those that remain is problematic, since they were recorded on nitrate cellulose filmstock, which is inflammable and chemically unstable. The major collections include:

UNITED STATES
Library of Congress
Motion Picture,
Broadcasting, and
Recorded Sound Division
Washington, DC 20540
Includes collection of paper prints of films that producers deposited to serve as copyright and to prevent counterfeiting

Museum of Modern Art
Department of Film
11 West 53 Street
New York, NY 10019

National Center for Film
and Video Preservation
American Film Institute
P.O. Box 27999
2021 North Western
Avenue
Los Angeles, CA 90027

Pacific Film Archive
University Art Museum
2625 Durant Avenue
Berkeley, CA 94720

CANADA
Cinémathèque Québecoise
335 Boulevard de
Maisonneuve
Montreal, Quebec
H2X IKI

ENGLAND
The Imperial War
Museum
Department of Film
Lambeth Road
London SEI 6HZ

National Film Archive
British Film Institute
21 Stephen Street
London WIP IPL

FRANCE
Cinémathèque Française
Palais de Chaillot
Avenue Albert-de-Mun
75016 Paris
Includes a museum and libraries of stills and books

Service des Archives du
Film du Centre National
de la Cinématographie
7 bis rue Alexandre-
Turpault
78390 Bois-d'Arcy
Includes a collection of equipment and posters

Film Museums

UNITED STATES
American Museum of the
Moving Image
3601 35th Avenue
Astoria, NY 11106

ENGLAND
The Museum of the
Moving Image
South Bank
London SEI 8SJ

National Museum of
Photography
Film and Television
Prince's View
Bradford, West Yorkshire
BD5 OTR

FRANCE
Musée Henri-Langlois
Cinémathèque Française
Palais de Chaillot
Avenue Albert-de-Mun
75016 Paris

Musée d'Orsay
1 rue de Bellechasse
75007 Paris

ITALY
Museo Nazionale del
Cinema
Palazzo Chiablese
Piazza San Giovanni 2
10122 Turin

Further Reading

Abel, Richard, *The Ciné Goes to Town*, University of California Press, Berkeley, 1994

Bandy, Mary Lea, ed., *Rediscovering French Film*, Museum of Modern Art/New York Graphic Society, New York, 1983

Barnes, John, *The Beginnings of Cinema in England*, Barnes & Noble, New York, 1976

Bitzer, G. W., *Billy Bitzer: His Story*, Farrar, Straus & Giroux, New York, 1973

Burch, Noël, *Life to Those Shadows*, trans. and ed. by Ben Brewster, University of California Press, Berkeley, 1993

Chanan, Michael, *The Dream That Kicks: The Prehistory and Early Years of Cinema in Britain*, Routledge & Kegan Paul, London, 1980

Cinema 1900–1906: An Analytical Study, 2 vols., FIAF, Brussels, 1982

Crafton, Donald, *Before Mickey: The Animated Film 1898–1928*, MIT Press, Cambridge, Mass., 1982

Elsaesser, Thomas, with Adam Barker, eds., *Early Cinema: Space—Frame—Narrative*, British Film Institute, London, 1990

Fell, John, et al., *Before Hollywood: Turn of the Century American Film*, Hudson Hills Press, New York, 1987

Frazer, John, *Artificially Arranged Scenes: The Films of Georges Méliès*, G. K. Hall, Boston, 1979

Garçon, François, *Gaumont: A Century of French Cinema*, Abrams, New York, 1994

Gomery, Douglas, *Shared Pleasures: A History of Movie Presentation in the United States*, University of Wisconsin Press, Madison, 1992

Guy, Alice, *Autobiographie d'Une Pionnière du Cinéma*, Denoël, Paris, 1975

Hammond, Paul, *Marvelous Méliès*, St. Martin's Press, New York, 1974

Hepworth, Cecil M., *Came the Dawn: Memories of a Film Pioneer*, Phoenix House Limited, London, 1951

Low, Rachel and R. Manvell, eds., *The History of British Film*, vol. I: 1896–1906, Allen & Unwin, London, 1948

Malthête-Méliès, Madeleine, *Méliès l'Enchanteur*, Malthête-Méliès, Paris, 1985

Mast, Gerald, *A Short History of the Movies*, Macmillan, New York, 1992

Michelson, Annette, et al., *The Art of Moving Shadows*, National Gallery of Art, Washington, D.C., 1989

Musser, Charles, *Before the Nickelodeon: Edwin S. Porter and the Edison Manufacturing Company*, University of California Press, Berkeley, 1991

————, *The Emergence of Cinema: The American Screen to 1907*, Scribners, New York, 1990

158 Scénarios de Films Disparus de Georges Méliès, Association Les Amis de Georges Méliès, Paris, 1986

Ramsaye, Terry, *A Million and One Nights: A History of the Motion Picture through 1925*, Simon & Schuster, New York, 1926

Rawlence, Christopher, *Missing Reel: Le Prince*, Collins, London, 1990

Salt, Barry, *Film Style and Technology: History and Analysis*, Starword, London, 1992

Sklar, Robert, *Film: An International History of the Medium*, Abrams, New York, 1993

Chronology

16th century	Painters and engravers use a camera obscura investigated by Leonardo da Vinci (It., 1452–1519)
1646	Jesuit priest Athanasius Kircher (Ger., 1601–80) describes a magic lantern in *Ars Magna Lucis et Umbrae*
1798	Etienne Gaspar Robert, known as Robertson (Belg., 1763–1837), presents his first Phantasmagoria shows using an enhanced magic lantern
1826	Joseph Nicéphore Niepce (Fr., 1765–1833) takes the first still photograph using a kind of camera obscura The Thaumatrope, devised by Dr. John Ayrton Paris (GB), blurs the images on two sides of a round card into a single image when spun by an attached string
1829	Joseph Plateau (Belg., 1801–83) first writes about the phenomenon of persistence of vision
1833	Plateau invents the Phenakistoscope, a slotted disk that resynthesizes continuous motion
1834	Mathematician William George Horner (GB, 1786–1837) devises the Daedelum (renamed Zoetrope), a bowl-shaped version of the Phenakistoscope
1837	Louis-Jacques-Mandé Daguerre (Fr., 1789–1851) invents the daguerreotype, which fixes images on a silver-covered copper plate
1839	Henry Langdon Childe (GB) introduces dissolving views, an enhanced magic lantern effect
1853	Baron Franz von Uchatius (Aus.) projects images onto a screen by combining a phenakistoscopic disk with a magic lantern
1864	Louis Arthur Ducos de Haron (Fr., 1837–1920) patents (but never builds) a 3600-lens camera designed to record successive images
1873	Eadweard James Muybridge (GB, 1830–1904) contrives a photographic apparatus to analyze the motion of a trotting horse
1874	Astronomer Pierre-Jules-Cesar Janssen (Fr., 1824–1907) devises a photographic mechanism to record the transit of Venus across the sun
1877	Emile Reynaud (Fr., 1844–1918) invents the Praxinoscope, an improved Zoetrope Muybridge publishes his sequences of stop-action photographs of horses, taken by setting up a battery of twelve (later expanded to twenty-four, then forty-eight) cameras
1878	Thomas Alva Edison (US, 1847–1931) invents the phonograph
1879	Photographers use gelatin plates sensitized with bromide of silver Ferrier works on roll film and coats a flexible gelatin strip with a gelatin-bromide emulsion Muybridge's Zoogyroscope (an improved Zoetrope) reconstitutes motion captured by his stop-action photographs

1880	Reynaud invents the projecting Praxinoscope
1881	Muybridge creates the Zoopraxiscope, a refined Zoogyroscope Louis Lumière (Fr., 1864–1948) perfects his blue label photographic plate
1882	Etienne-Jules Marey (Fr., 1830–1904) devises a photographic gun to record sequential images and invents a fixed-plate chronophotographic camera
1883	Albert Londe (Fr., 1858–1917) uses his multiple-lens camera at the Hôpital de la Salpêtrière
1886	Louis Aimé Augustin Le Prince (Fr., 1841–90) patents a multiple-lens camera using paper filmstrips
1887	Hannibal Goodwin (US) invents flexible cellulose nitrate-based roll film Marey invents a chronophotograph that uses paper roll film Muybridge publishes *Animal Locomotion (Animals in Motion, The Human Figure in Motion)* Ottomar Anschütz (Ger., 1846–1907) presents his Electrotachyscope to Berlin audiences
1888	Edison and William Kennedy Laurie Dickson (US, 1860–1937) build an optical cylindrical phonograph Reynaud patents his Théâtre Optique
1889	George Eastman (US, 1854–1932) develops and markets flexible cellulose nitrate roll film Edison and Dickson order batches of film from Eastman and perforate the strips William Friese-Greene (GB, 1855–1921) records animated photographs with a chronophotographic camera
1891	Georges Démeny (Fr., 1850–1917) invents the Phonoscope, designed to resynthesize lip movement for deaf-mutes Edison and Dickson patent a motion-picture camera (Kinetograph) and an individual viewing machine (Kinetoscope)
1892	Edison, Dickson, and Eugène Lauste (Fr., 1856–1935) work on the Kinetophone, an early combination kinetoscope and phonograph Léon Bouly (Fr., 1872–1932) patents the Cinématographe, a camera that both analyzes and resynthesizes motion Reynaud presents his Théâtre Optique and projects his "Luminous Pantomimes" at the Musée Grévin, Paris
1893	Acme LeRoy (US, 1854–1944) and Lauste invent the Marvelous Cinematograph, a Kinetoscope projector Démeny builds a Chronophotograph with a cam mechanism Edison's Black Maria, the world's first motion-picture studio, is built Kinetoscope Company founded by Norman Raff and Frank Gammon
1894	Dickson shoots his first films for Kinetoscope Opening of the first Kinetoscope parlors in New York and London First demonstration of LeRoy and Lauste's Marvelous Cinematograph projector in New York Working with Woodville Latham (US, 1838–1911) and his sons Gray and Otway, Lauste invents the Panoptikon (renamed Eidoloscope), a new type of Kinetoscope projector

Woodville Latham invents the so-called Latham loop, a small loop of excess film, which prevents tearing

Max Skladanowsky (Ger., 1863–1939) builds his Bioskop and shoots short scenes

Charles Pathé (Fr., 1863–1957) exhibits Edison phonographs at fairgrounds

Louis Lumière invents a new feed mechanism; his chief engineer, Charles Moisson, is asked to build the prototype of a machine to shoot, print, and project motion pictures

1895 | Lumière patents the Cinématographe

Lumière shoots *Workers Leaving the Lumière Factory* and other films

First private demonstrations of Lumière's Cinématographe

Robert W. Paul (GB, 1869–1943) builds counterfeit Kinetoscopes. Working with Birt Acres (GB, 1854–1918), he develops the Animatograph (or Theatrograph) camera and shoots his first films

Pathé exhibits counterfeit Kinetoscopes purchased from Paul

Pathé teams up with Henri Joly (Fr., 1866–1945), who builds a multipeephole Kinetoscope and a camera

Thomas Armat (US, 1866–1948) and Charles Francis Jenkins (US, 1867–1934) invent the Phantascope, a Kinetoscope projector

Edison gains control of the Armat patents and markets the projector as the Vitascope

First public performance of Skladanowsky's Bioskop projector at the Wintergarden, Berlin

Dickson, Herman Casler, Harry Marvin, and Elias Bernard Koopman form the American Mutoscope Company

Mutoscope built

The Cinématographe Lumière opens to the public in the Salon Indien of the Grand Café, Paris

1896 | Lumière's Cinématographe filming worldwide

Paul's Theatrograph debuts at the Egyptian Hall, London

First Vitascope screening for a paying audience at Koster & Bial's Music Hall, New York

Jules Carpenter builds a series of Lumière cinematographs

Auguste Baron (Fr., 1855–1938) invents a process for making sound pictures

Pathé Frères founded by Charles Pathé and brothers Emile, Jacques, and Théophile

Léon Gaumont (Fr., 1864–1946) comes out with his 60-mm Démeny Chronophotographe

Biograph camera built

Screening of first Biograph films

Georges Méliès (Fr., 1861–1938) shoots his first films, including *The Vanishing Lady*

1897 | A 60-mm Joly-Normandin projector causes a fire, killing 140

Méliès builds a studio at Montreuil-sous-Bois

Gaumont comes out with his 35-mm Gaumont-Démeny Chronophotographe

Gaumont's secretary, Alice Guy (Fr., 1873–1968), shoots her first films

J. Stuart Blackton (US, 1875–1941) and Albert E. Smith found the Vitagraph Company

Paul forms Paul's Animatograph Works, Ltd.

George Albert Smith (GB, 1864–1959) and James Williamson (GB, 1855–1933) shoot their first films in Brighton

1898 | Edison fires the opening shots in the "War of the Patents"

Charles Urban (US, 1871–1942) forms the Warwick Trading Company in London

The battleship *Maine* is blown up in Havana harbor, triggering the Spanish-American War and inspiring the first historical reconstruction films

Multiple-shot films by Méliès and Paul introduced

1899	Méliès's *The Dreyfus Affair*
	Newsreel-type films of action, both live and reenacted, shot of Transvaal during the Boer War
1900	Eighteen film-projection attractions at the Paris Universal Exposition include Lumière's giant-screen Cinématographe, the Cinéorama of Raoul Grimoin-Sanson (Fr., 1860–1941), the Phonorama, and the Phono-Cinema-Théâtre
	Smith's *Grandma's Reading Glass*
	Williamson's *Attack on a China Mission Station*
1901	Williamson's *The Big Swallow* and *Stop Thief!*
	Crime Story by Ferdinand Zecca (Fr., 1864–1947)
1902	Pathé Studios built at Vincennes
	Gaumont demonstrates his Phonoscènes (talking films) to the Société Française de Photographie
	Méliès's *A Trip to the Moon*
	Méliès's *The Coronation of Edward VII*
	Zecca's *The Victims of Alcoholism*
	Urban forms the Charles Urban Trading Company
	The Life of an American Fireman by Edwin S. Porter (US, 1870–1941)
1903	Porter's *The Great Train Robbery*
1904	Hale's Tours opens at the St. Louis World's Fair
	Newsreel-type films of action, both live and reconstructed, during the Russo-Japanese War
	Chase films increasingly popular
1905	Stencil coloring of films begins
	Gaumont Studios built in Paris
	Rescued by Rover by Cecil Hepworth (GB, 1873–1953)
	First Italian fiction film, *La Presa di Roma*, by Filoteo Alberini (It., 1865–1937)
1906	Smith patents Kinemacolor, a two-color filmmaking process
	Oskar Messter (Ger., 1866–1943) develops a system for making sound films
	Development of Gaumont's Chronophone
	The Vitagraph Company of America opens a new studio in Brooklyn; the American Mutoscope and Biograph Company opens a West Coast office in Los Angeles
	Nickelodeons spring up across the United States
	Formation of Cinés film company in Italy and Nordisk Films Compagni in Denmark
	Blackton's *Humorous Phases of Funny Faces*
	Méliès's *The Merry Frolics of Satan*
	Alice Guy's *The Life of Christ*

List of Illustrations

Index

Acknowledgements

The publishers would like to thank the following people and institutions for their help in the preparation of this book: Aldo Bernardini, Vicenza; Marie Borel, Noëlle Giret, Christine Petitot, Cinémathèque Française, Paris; Amanzio Borio, Museo Nazionale del Cinema, Turin; Eileen Bowser, MOMA, New York; Bernard Chardère, Institut Lumière, Lyon; Yasha David, Paris; Frédérique Desvergnes, CNAM, Paris; M. Dimitrio, Cinémathèque Suisse, Lausanne; Maxine Ducey, State Historical Society of Wisconsin, Madison; Claire Espilondo, FIAF 50, Paris; David Francis, British Film Institute, London; André Gaudreault, Suzanne Richard, GRAF, Laval University, Québec; Maurice Gianati, Paris; Jeanne Guillevic, Mme. Salvador, Musée Dupuy, Toulouse; Institut Jean-Vigo, Perpignan; International Federation of Film Archives, Brussels; Wolfgang Klaue, Staatliches Filmarchiv der DDR, Berlin; Library of the Institut Catholique, Paris; Madeleine Malthête–Méliès, Jacques Malthète, Paris; Miguel Marias, Filmoteca Española, Madrid; Michel Marie; Eva Orbanz, Berlin; Pierre Pitrou, photographer, Paris; Sylvie Pliskin, Cinémathèque Universitaire, Paris; Franz and Nicole Schmitt, Service des Archives de Film, Bois-d'Arcy; Science Museum Library, London; Tom Smith, American Federation of Arts, New York; Paul Spehr, Library of Congress, Washington; Giuseppe Valperga, Turin. Frédéric Dumas compiled the illustrations for this work and Pierre Pitrou photographed numerous documents. I. Mark Paris contributed invaluable research and translation assistance.

Photograph Credits

All rights reserved 20–1, 23a, 28, 29, 31, 37a, 41b, 45, 47, 54a, 54bl, 59b, 71, 80, 93, 103b, 109, 122–3, 127a, 131, 160–1; American Federation of Arts, New York 90, 91b; Archives du Film, Bois-d'Arcy 76; British Film Institute, London 1, 4, 5a, 6, 7, 8, 9, 26, 44l, 74, 75b, 94–5, 96–7, 98, 102, 104, 108, 112, 113, 114–5, 116, 117, 118–9, 120, 124–5, 125, 126, 127b, 142, 148–9, 152, 154, 171; British Film Institute (with the authorization of the Georges Méliès copyright holders) 62b, 101a; Cinémathèque Française, Paris 12, 13, 14a, 15, 16, 17b, 18, 19a, 19b, 21, 22, 23b, 24–5, 30–1, 32, 33, 34a, 36–7, 43, 44b, 46, 50a, 53, 57, 59a, 70, 77, 78–9, 79, 81, 100–1, 101b, 103a, 110, 111, 115, 121; Cinémathèque Française (with the authorization of the Georges Méliès copyright holders) back cover, 60b, 62b, 64b, 65, 88, 89, 141, 157, 159; Cinémathèque Suisse, Lausanne 37b; Cinémathèque Universitaire, Paris 5b, 73a; Cinéplus 42, 49b; Cineteca Española, Madrid 72–3, 73b; Collection Gianati, Pierre Pitrou stills, Paris 82, 83, 84, 85, 86, 87; Collection Malthête-Méliès, Paris 52, 61, 63, 64b, 66, 67, 68, 69, 99; Institut Jean-Vigo, Perpignan 2, 3; Institut Lumière, Lyon 17a, 24, 27, 40–1, 134; Musée de la Publicité, Paris 75, 54br; Musée National des Arts et Traditions Populaires, Paris 51, 75a; Musée National des Techniques, CNAM, Paris 41a, 105, 140; Museo Nazionale del Cinema, Turin 14b, 25, 56, 58; Museum of Modern Art, New York front cover, 34b, 35r, 38, 60a, 91a, 92, 106, 107; Roger-Viollet 49a; Staatliches Filmarchiv der DDR, Berlin 39, 48; State Historical Society of Wisconsin, Madison 55

Text Credits

Grateful acknowlegment is made for use of material from the following sources: G. W. Bitzer, "Filming My First War: 1898" from *Billy Bitzer: His Story*. Copyright © 1973 by Ethel Bitzer. Reprinted by permission of Farrar, Straus & Giroux, Inc. (pp. 152–5); Alice Guy, *Autobiographie d'une pionnière du cinéma (1873–1968)* Denoël/Gonthier, 1976, translated by Andrew Litvack. Reprinted by permission (pp. 150–1); Cecil M. Hepworth, *Came the Dawn: Memories of a Film Pioneer*, J. M. Dent & Sons, Publishers (pp. 146–8); "Lumière, the Last Interview," *Sight and Sound*, Summer 1948. Reprinted by courtesy of the British Film Institute (pp. 134–7); Terry Ramsaye, *A Million and One Nights: A History of the Motion Picture*, published by Simon & Schuster. Reprinted by permission of Mrs. Terry Ramsaye (p. 156)

Emmanuelle Toulet is a curator in the Department of
Entertainment Arts at the Bibliothèque Nationale in Paris,
where she is in charge of the film collection. She has
published several articles, principally on the history of
French silent films and on safeguarding our
cinematographic heritage.

Translated from the French by Susan Emanuel

This book was produced with the kind collaboration of the member
cinematheques of the International Federation of Film Archives (FIAF) in Brussels

Editor: Sharon AvRutick
Typographic Designer: Elissa Ichiyasu
Design Supervisor: Miko McGinty
Design Assistant: Tina Thompson
Text Permissions: Neil Ryder Hoos

Library of Congress Catalog Card Number: 94–77942

ISBN 0–8109–2874–4

Copyright © 1988 Gallimard/Réunion des Musées Nationaux

English translation copyright © 1995 Harry N. Abrams, Inc., New York,
and Thames and Hudson Ltd., London

Published in 1995 by Harry N. Abrams, Inc., New York
A Times Mirror Company

Printed and bound in Italy by Editoriale Libraria, Trieste